Praise for *The Executive Guide to Information Security*

"*Every CEO is responsible for protecting the assets of their corporation—the people, intellectual property, corporate and customer information, infrastructure, network, and computing resources. This is becoming both more important and more difficult with the rise in the number and sophistication of cyber threats. This book helps the CEO understand the issues and ask the right questions to implement a more effective strategy for their business.*"
—Steve Bennett, president and CEO, Intuit

"*Mark Egan and Tim Mather help nontechnical executives gain a comprehensive perspective on the security challenges that all companies face today. This book is well structured and practical. Yet, it also stresses that a strategic approach to cyber security is essential, and that "tone at the top" will determine the effectiveness of any corporate cyber security policy.*"
—Eric Benhamou, chairman of the board of directors, 3Com Corporation, palmOne, and PalmSource, Inc.

"*This book is not about cyber security; it's about managing one's company and the role that cyber security plays in that scenario. It's chilling to think of how vulnerable the assets of a business are on a computer network; this book is a fire alarm in the night for business executives to realize computer security is not a tech issue—it's a business issue worthy of the same attention and priority that business executives might place on any other mission-critical element of their company.*"
—George Reyes, CFO, Google

"*This is a must read for any executive of any size company. The Internet makes all businesses equal in that they are subject to the same types of threats regardless of their product. In this book, the CIO and security director of one of the top security companies makes the business case for security and tells you what to do to successfully mitigate threats.*"
—Howard A. Schmidt, former cyber security advisor to the White House, CSO Microsoft, and VP CISO eBay

D1378598

THE EXECUTIVE GUIDE TO

INFORMATION SECURITY

THE EXECUTIVE GUIDE TO

INFORMATION SECURITY

THREATS, CHALLENGES, AND SOLUTIONS

MARK EGAN
with Tim Mather

✦✦ Addison-Wesley

Indianapolis

Many of the designations used by manufacturers and sellers to distinguish their products are claimed as trademarks. Where those designations appear in this book, and the publisher was aware of a trademark claim, the designations have been printed with initial capital letters or in all capitals.

The authors and publisher have taken care in the preparation of this book but make no expressed or implied warranty of any kind and assume no responsibility for errors or omissions. No liability is assumed for incidental or consequential damages in connection with or arising out of the use of the information or programs contained herein.

Publisher Symantec Press: Linda McCarthy
Editor in Chief: Karen Gettman
Acquisitions Editor: Jessica Goldstein
Cover Designer: Alan Clements
Managing Editor: Gina Kanouse
Project Editor: Christy Hackerd
Copy Editor: Ben Lawson
Indexer: Lisa Stumpf
Proofreader: Karen A. Gill
Senior Compositor: Gloria Schurick
Manufacturing Buyer: Dan Uhrig

The publisher offers excellent discounts on this book when ordered in quantity for bulk purchases or special sales, which may include electronic versions and/or custom covers and content particular to your business, training goals, marketing focus, and branding interests. For more information, please contact:

U. S. Corporate and Government Sales
(800) 382-3419
corpsales@pearsontechgroup.com

For sales outside the U. S., please contact:

International Sales
international@pearsoned.com

Visit us on the web: www.awprofessional.com

Library of Congress Cataloging-in-Publication Data:

2004111877

ISBN 0-32-130451-9

Text printed in the United States at *Courier Corporation in Stoughton, Massachusetts.*
Third printing, *March 2005*

To Sophie, Nicholas, and Danielle

Table of Contents

Acknowledgments

Special thanks go to Tim Mather, who worked closely with me over the past two years and explained the finer points of information security, drafted portions of the book, and reviewed countless changes to the manuscript. Tim also served as the technical expert on information security for the book. We would not have completed the project without his hard work.

I would also like to thank Linda McCarthy from Symantec Press, who was instrumental in finalizing the manuscript and putting the finishing touches on the book to get it published. My appreciation goes to Jessica Goldstein from Addison Wesley, who streamlined the publishing process and enabled us to complete the project in record time.

I am grateful to Becky Ranninger and Derek Witte, who read an early draft of the manuscript and offered comments that were fundamental in shaping the book. Joe Feliu reviewed several drafts of the book, and I want to thank him for providing considerable insight and suggestions.

I would like to thank Richard Clarke, who was kind enough to write the Foreword to my book, and Eric Benhamou, Steve Bennett, George Reyes, and Howard Schmidt, who took the time to review my book and provide quotes.

Thanks to my friend Harris Kern, who came up with the idea for this book and encouraged me to write it. I must also extend my thanks to Barbara Rhodes, who did an outstanding job of turning my scribbles into charts and graphs, and Karen Myer, who helped wrap up the final edits.

Acknowledgments

Many friends and colleagues took time from their busy lives and helped on the book in various stages of completion, and I wish to thank them (they are listed in alphabetical order): Jim Cates, Bob Concannon, Rob Clyde, Robert Corpuz, Art Courville, Richard Diamond, Shobana Gubbi, Brian Hernacki, Bill Ihrie, Dean Lane, Marina Levinson, Jack McCullough, John Moreno, Cris Paden, Dave Schwartz, Steve Trilling, and Angella Wilger.

I would also like to thank my parents, Tom and Dorothy Egan, who instilled a strong work ethic in me that has served me well over my fortunate career.

Finally, I would like to thank my wife Sophie for her sound advice and encouragement during this project. She allowed me to free up time to devote to the book, and I will be forever indebted to her.

Mark Egan
November 21, 2004
Los Altos, California

Foreword

One of the most difficult challenges I faced as the head of the President's Critical Infrastructure Protection Board (PCIPB) was communicating the complexities of Internet security to the public and private officials I dealt with on a day-to-day basis.

My challenge was to explain why Internet security was so important but to do it in a way that wouldn't cause people's eyes to glaze over within five minutes. I had to explain things in a compelling way in the limited time I had with them so that when I walked out of that room, an impression would have been made in their minds that would carry over into their everyday operations afterwards.

At the time, a book like *The Executive Guide to Information Security: Threats, Challenges, and Solutions* by Mark Egan of Symantec would have been tremendously useful and helpful.

I had the pleasure of working closely with Symantec and their people on many different issues during my tenure at the PCIPB, particularly in the formation of the National Strategy to Secure Cyberspace.

That plan shared many of the same goals and messages as this book, primarily that Internet security is a necessity for users in the home and at work—not a luxury. Computer security is an issue that CEOs in particular must realize is as imperative as any of their business operations. If times are tight, the last place you want to cut is the area of securing one's cybernetwork.

In today's interconnected world, no business can operate without securing its computers any more than it would try to operate without an accountant or a legal department. Cybersecurity is that imperative.

Unfortunately, many CEOs fail to grasp that fact until after their business has become a victim of cyberattack, be it hacking or virus infection.

Mark's book conveys that message in clear, concise terms and acts as a tremendous primer to CEOs on why cybersecurity is important and what factors they need to consider when putting a plan together to protect their computer networks.

As we all know, CEOs are extremely busy and don't have the time to conduct in-depth research on the issues, so they need practical recommendations that can be implemented quickly.

This book is devoted to executives who could benefit from a crash course on computer security through concepts that are explained in terms that are non-technical and easy to understand.

The book provides a pragmatic approach for evaluating the security of a computer network for a business and how to develop an encompassing enterprise information security program. Key elements of such a program include staffing, implementing processes and procedures, and installing appropriate technology.

The challenge that this nation faces as far as securing its cyberinfrastructure cannot be overstated. Computer networks governing our financial institutions, emergency response systems, and power grids are just a few entities of many that are tremendously vulnerable to cyberattack or disruptive viruses.

It's a challenge that must be met by all of us, both in the public and private sector. More importantly, cybersecurity is a responsibility that must be accepted by CEOs as an issue that they must be intimately involved with, not something to be delegated and updated on once a quarter. Because of the complexity and aggressiveness of today's cyberattacks, CEOs of businesses of all sizes have a role in securing not only their own computer networks but indirectly the infrastructure of our country as a whole.

Therefore, if you are a CEO who grasps this concept and understands what's at stake, I recommend that you read this book. If your time truly is money, I can't think of a better investment than *The Executive Guide to Information Security: Threats, Challenges, and Solutions.*

—Richard Clarke, former chairman of the President's Critical Infrastructure Protection Board and former special advisor to the President for Cyber Security

Preface

Who Is This Book For

This book is devoted to executives who could benefit from a crash course on information security. We know that you are quite busy, so you need practical recommendations that you can implement quickly. In this book, information security concepts are explained in nontechnical terms to enable executives from any discipline to quickly understand key principles and how to apply them to their business.

This book provides a pragmatic approach to evaluating security at your company and putting together an information security program. Key elements of the program include staffing this function at your company, putting the necessary internal processes in place, and implementing the appropriate technology. Business executives will find this book a good primer for understanding the key existing and future security issues and for taking the necessary actions to ensure the protection of their enterprise's information assets.

Information Security Background

Information security is no longer an issue that is the responsibility of lower-level staff in the information technology (IT) department. Companies are now conducting a significant portion of their business electronically and need to be confident that their systems are safe and secure. This issue has now been escalated to the Board of Director level, and companies need to take information security seriously.

The passage of the Sarbanes-Oxley Act has caused boards and especially audit committees to get much more involved in monitoring the performance and security of key information systems. This act requires companies to make new disclosures about internal controls and includes significant penalties and possible prison terms for executives of companies that are not in compliance.

When I started with Symantec in 1999, information security was slowly becoming a major issue that executives had to address. More business was being conducted on the Internet, and system outages gained much more attention from the media. Many companies did not have formal information security programs, and security issues were addressed in an "ad hoc" fashion. Technology solutions at that time consisted mainly of firewalls and anti-virus software that operated independently.

One of my challenges with my new position was to quickly gain an understanding of information security because Symantec had shifted its focus to address this market. Most of the literature that was available was very technical and did not provide a good overview for executives of how to put an effective information security program in place. Considering that I had spent the prior 25 years working in information technology, this would have been even more difficult for executives from other disciplines to understand.

The industry has changed considerably over the past few years, and a simple virus that was a minor annoyance in the past has shifted to major threats such as Code Red that have caused major disruptions to businesses. Unfortunately, the future does not hold much promise for things to improve, and businesses will need to devote much more attention to this area.

The objective of this book is to provide a shortcut for executives to learn more about information security and how it will affect their business in the future. An overview of information security concepts is provided so that executives can be better prepared to evaluate how their company is addressing information security. Pragmatic approaches are provided to assist companies in improving their information security programs.

How This Book Is Organized

This book focuses on three key themes: people, processes, and technology. These are the key elements of an effective information security program, and it is important to balance these components of the program. Considerable attention has been given to technology in the media and information security literature. However, this is just one element of an effective overall program. The best technology is not going to help if you do not have good staff and processes in place.

This book is organized according to the steps you would follow to develop an information security program for your company. Chapter 1, "The Information Security Challenge," provides an overview of information security challenges and why executives should pay attention to the potential risks that these challenges pose to their business. A historical review of the Internet and information security incidents is also covered, and the chapter offers some insight into the power and vulnerability of conducting business electronically.

Chapter 2, "Information Security Overview," provides an introduction to information security and the key elements of an effective program. The Security Evaluation Framework is introduced in Chapter 3, "Developing Your Information Security Program," and can be used to evaluate your information security program and develop a roadmap to improve your program. The overall methodology is reviewed, along with the critical areas to ensure success. The next three chapters are devoted to evaluating the people, process, and technology components of your information security program and developing an improvement plan. Chapter 7, "Information Security Roadmap," pulls all this analysis together and describes how to develop your roadmap to an improved information security program that is appropriate for your company.

Future trends for information security are reviewed in Chapter 8, "View into the Future," which offers some insight into emerging threats and industry solutions to address these threats. This field is changing rapidly, and it is important to always keep up to date on the latest events. The final chapter lists the 10 essential components to an effective information security program and offers a good summary for anyone who wants to quickly identify areas for improvement. Additional sources of information and references are included in the appendixes.

One final point is that this book is written from a vendor-neutral perspective; it does not contain references to commercially available security products and services. The focus is on industry best practices for information security. Due to the rapid changes in this industry, it is difficult to predict which companies will lead as the market evolves. The concepts outlined in this book can serve as a guide to choosing the appropriate products and services to support your program today and in the future.

About the Authors

Mark Egan is Symantec's chief information officer and vice president of information technology. He is responsible for the management of Symantec's internal business systems, computing infrastructure, and information security program. Egan led the rapid transformation of Symantec's internal information systems over the past four years, as the company grew to be the leader in Internet security. Egan brings more than 25 years of information technology experience from a variety of industries. Prior to Symantec, he held several senior-level positions with companies including Sun Microsystems, Price Waterhouse, Atlantic Richfield Corp., Martin Marietta Data Systems, and Wells Fargo Bank. He is a member of the American Management Association's Information Systems and Technology Council and serves on the technical advisory boards for Golden Gate University and the Center for Electronic Business at San Francisco State University. Egan is also co-chair of TechNet's Cyber Security Practices Adoption Campaign. Egan was a contributing author to *CIO Wisdom* and is a frequent speaker on best practices for information technology and information security.

Egan holds a master's degree in finance and international business from the University of San Diego and a bachelor's degree in computer sciences from the University of Clarion.

Tim Mather is Symantec's vice president and chief information security officer and is a Certified Information Systems Security Professional (CISSP) and a Certified Information Systems Manager (CISM). As the chief information security officer, he is responsible for the development of all information systems security policies, oversight of implementation of all security-related policies and procedures, and all information systems audit-related activities. He also works closely with internal products groups on security capabilities in Symantec products. Prior to joining Symantec in September 1999, Mather was the manager of security at VeriSign. In addition, he was formerly manager of information systems security at Apple Computer. Mather's experience also includes seven years in Washington, D.C. working on secure communications for a classified, national-level command, control, communications, and intelligence (C^3I) project, which involved both civilian and military departments and agencies.

Mather holds master's degrees in national security studies from Georgetown University and international policy studies from Monterey Institute of International Studies. He holds a bachelor's degree in political economics from the University of California at Berkeley.

Chapter 1
The Information Security Challenge

Four CEOs were taking a break during a recent American Banking Association (ABA) meeting and struck up a conversation about recent challenges they were facing. Howard related a recent incident caused by the Slammer Worm that made his bank's 13,000 automated teller machines (ATMs) unavailable to their customers for approximately 24 hours. This worm spread so quickly that his information technology (IT) organization could not react in time. A worm is a self-replicating malicious program that doesn't require user interaction to spread between computers and across networks. Fast-replicating worms can consume resources, slowing computers and networks to a crawl or crashing them altogether.

Sam could relate to Howard's woes because someone stole a laptop computer that contained private financial information for thousands of customers from one of his bank's offices. Sam's business was lucky and recovered the laptop a few days later; however, his customer service organization spent considerable time contacting these customers and continues to monitor their accounts for possible fraud.

Roger was not so lucky. An eastern European hacker tricked his company's systems into transferring an estimated $10 million into the hacker's account. His bank was able to recover the majority of these funds, but the incident did considerable damage to his company's brand. Charles lamented the damage to his credit card business when hackers sent phony but official-looking emails (a process called "phishing") to his unsuspecting customers to trick them into disclosing confidential information. These hackers then made illegal charges to the accounts of customers who fell for the scam.

The preceding anecdotes are based upon actual recent security incidents that have occurred in the financial services industry. Information security incidents are not limited to this industry, however. All organizations that conduct portions of their business electronically are potential targets. In April 2003, the Slammer Worm disabled a safety monitoring system at a nuclear power plant for nearly five hours and affected the performance of the plant's corporate network. A major U.S. computer networking company sued a Chinese rival for theft of intellectual property in January 2003. The company claimed that its rival copied its source code, documentation, and other copyrighted information. Both parties settled 20 months later when the Chinese rival agreed to discontinue selling all products named in the lawsuit.

In December 1999, an online music distributor refused to hand over a $100,000 blackmail payment when a hacker stole the confidential personal information, including credit card numbers, of 350,000 of their customers. The hacker posted the information on the Internet, and the resulting brand damage was severe. Finally, two software companies in the Silicon Valley have been embroiled in a billion dollar lawsuit over the theft of intellectual property that allegedly resulted when executives from one of the companies left to form a competitive company.

A lack of knowledge about information security contributed to these incidents and left these companies vulnerable to exploitation. This book explains how you can avoid the same trap and provides you with the resources and best practices necessary to put the information to good use.

Introduction

Information security is a significant boardroom issue. In today's world, companies rely on their internal computer systems and the Internet to conduct business and cannot afford to have disruptions to their operations. A security incident can have a wide-ranging negative impact on a company's revenue streams, customer confidence, and public relations. This dilemma makes information security an essential component to an effective overall business strategy. Establishing an information security program that addresses the risks that your business faces should be a high priority.

Overview

This chapter starts with a historical view of the Internet that provides important and relevant background information for understanding information security. It goes on to describe some of the major information security challenges that you're likely to face and how they can affect your business. These challenges are important to consider when developing your information security program, and you can turn them into competitive advantages.

Understanding the Internet—A Brief History

What is the *Internet*? The Internet is a global network of computer networks. Each network might contain thousands of computers that are connected or *networked* together. The term internet is short for internetwork or interconnected network; when capitalized, the term refers to the global internetwork or *Internet*, which enables millions of computers to communicate with each other on a daily basis.

The Internet was originally intended to be ubiquitous, and it was assumed that its users knew and trusted each other, which facilitated communication. However, as the popularity of the Internet grew, so did the number of users, which led to the deterioration of the trust model. This phenomenon completely changed the usage of the Internet, because users of the system were now at the mercy of a small number of individuals (who became known as *hackers*) who had the advanced skills needed to fully understand and manipulate the system. Some members of this newly formed community exploited the network's wide-open design for personal gain or bragging rights.

The popularity of the Internet continued to grow within the academic and government communities, but it did not extend to enterprises due to the technical skills required to access the system and commercial use restrictions. However, this all changed in the early 1990s with the development of Internet browsers such as Mosaic and Netscape Navigator. These advancements revolutionized the Internet, and now in addition to text, web pages contain graphics, pictures, sound, animation, and even video. The popularity of the Internet grew sharply after the advent of these browsers, as shown in Figure 1-1.

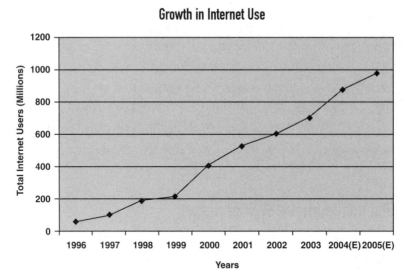

Figure 1-1   Internet growth.

The U.S. government also relaxed and later removed commercial use restrictions, and mainstream businesses started to use the Internet as another medium to communicate with their customers, which has now eclipsed the original objectives of sharing information among academic and government organizations.

Although the openness of the Internet enabled businesses to quickly adopt its technology ecosystem, it also proved to be a great weakness from an information security perspective. The system's original purpose as a means of collaboration between groups of trusted colleagues is no longer practical because the usage has expanded into millions of frequently anonymous users.

Numerous security incidents related to viruses, worms, and other malicious software have occurred since the Morris Worm, which was the first and shut down 10% of the systems on the Internet in 1988. These incidents have become increasingly complex and costly. Table 1-1 provides a brief overview of other major incidents over the past few years.

Table 1-1

Major Information Security Incidents

Name	Date	Impact
Morris Worm	1988	■ Stopped 10% of computers connected to Internet
Melissa Virus	May 1999	■ 100,000 computers in one week ■ $1.5 billion impact
Explorer Virus	June 1999	■ $1.1 billion impact
Love Bug Virus (I Love You Virus)	May 2000	■ $8.75 billion impact
Sircam Virus	July 2001	■ 2.3 million computers infected ■ $1.25 billion impact
Code Red Worm	July 2001	■ 359,000 computers infected in less than 14 hours ■ $2.75 billion impact
Nimda Worm	Sept. 2001	■ 160,000 computers infected at peak ■ $1.5 billion impact
Klez	2002	■ $750 million impact
BugBear	2002	■ $500 million impact
Badtrands	2002	■ $400 million impact
Sapphire/Slammer Worm	Jan. 2003	■ Infected 90% of vulnerable hosts in just 10 minutes ■ 75,000 hosts infected at peak ■ $1.5 billion impact
Blaster	2003	■ $750 million impact
Nachi	2003	■ $500 million impact
SoBig.F	2003	■ $2.5 billion impact
MyDoom Worm	Jan. 2004	■ Fastest spreading mass-mailer worm to date ■ 100,000 instances of the worm intercepted per hour ■ More than $4.0 billion impact

continues

Name	Date	Impact
Witty Worm	March 2004	■ First widely propagated worm to carry a destructive payload

*Sources: "Virus Costs on the Rise Again—2004 Update," Computer Economics, March 2004.
"MyDoom Virus Update; Fastest Spreading Virus Ever," Computer Economics, February 2004.
"The Spread of the Witty Worm—CAIDA ANALYSIS," Cooperative Association for Internet Data
Analysis (CAIDA), www.caida.org.*

The Internet has grown from just a few thousand users in 1983 to more than 800 million users worldwide in 2004. It provides a vital online channel to conduct business with existing and potential customers. However, despite this huge upside, the Internet poses significant security risks that businesses ignore or underestimate at their own peril. The following section describes the major information security challenges to businesses today.

Six Significant Information Security Challenges

Executives need to understand and address six significant challenges, which are listed here and reviewed in detail in the following sections:

- E-commerce requirements
- Information security attacks
- Immature information security market
- Information security staff shortage
- Government legislation and industry regulations
- Mobile workforce and wireless computing

Electronic Commerce

The Internet has created an important channel for conducting business called electronic commerce (e-commerce). This channel provides many new ways for businesses to offer products and services to their customers. In the past, the ability to connect with millions of customers 24 hours a day, 7 days a week was only possible for the largest corporations. Now even a company with limited resources can compete with larger rivals by offering products and services through the Internet with only a modest investment. E-commerce services are quite appealing to consumers who do not want to spend their limited free time in traditional retail stores constrained by normal business hours of operation, unfriendly staff, and long checkout lines. Executives must understand how to leverage this new channel of electronic commerce while managing the associated risks.

Companies now rely on the Internet to offer products and services according to their customer's buying preferences. The Internet is no longer an optional sales method but rather a vital distribution channel that a business cannot ignore. Figure 1-2 provides a summary of commerce conducted electronically in 2002.

Source: Morgan Stanley; The State of Retailing Online 6.0—2003 Shop.org survey conducted by Forrester Research, Inc.

Figure 1-2 Growth in electronic commerce.

Pioneering companies such as eBay and Amazon have revolutionized the easy purchase of products through the Internet. Not only is it easy for customers to purchase their products, but also companies have innovated the use of concepts such as "personalization" to create unique relationships with individual customers. Using personalization, companies are able to identify their online customers by name, offer products based upon previous buying habits, and safely store home address information to make purchasing online much quicker. These strategies have enabled successful e-commerce companies to create a positive shopping experience without the overhead associated with traditional retail stores.

Retail securities is another industry that has been transformed as a result of the Internet. In the past, a stockbroker might charge a few hundred dollars to trade a thousand shares of stock. Now a consumer can use an online brokerage firm and complete the same trade for less than twenty dollars. This has revolutionized the securities industry by providing a much more cost-effective service to their customers. It has also put a large number of retail stockbrokers out of work.

Along with increased capabilities come some new challenges that businesses must overcome to be successful. For instance:

- Companies are under tremendous pressure to deliver these systems as quickly as possible because being first to market with a new capability can be a great competitive advantage.

- Timely and accurate access to information for employees, customers, and partners is no longer nice to have—it is expected.

- Companies must offer these services in an easy-to-use but completely secure manner because they store confidential information such as home addresses and personal credit card numbers.

- The systems are expected to be available 24 hours a day, 7 days a week because customers expect to be able to access the products and services at their convenience, not the company's.

These challenges place considerable demands on IT organizations because delivering these e-commerce systems in a timely and secure manner is very difficult. As expectations increase, so do the demands on the systems and technology.

Constant Growth and Complexity of Information Security Attacks

Security incidents that are related to malicious code (worms, viruses, and Trojans) have grown from slightly annoying to significantly damaging to business operations. A computer virus is a piece of malicious code that attaches to or infects executable programs. Unlike worms, viruses rely on users to execute or launch an infected program to replicate or deliver their payloads. A virus' payload can delete data or damage system files.

A *Trojan* (named after the Trojan horse in Greek mythology) is a malicious program disguised as something innocuous, often a utility or screensaver. Like viruses, Trojans rely on unsuspecting users to activate them by launching the program to which the Trojan is attached. Trojans have many functions; some delete or steal data, whereas others install *backdoors* that enable a hacker to take control of a system. Unlike viruses, Trojans do not replicate.

Early computer viruses were often contained to individual users' systems, resulting in only a small decline in staff productivity for a given day. However, present-day *blended threats*, such as Code Red and Nimda, present multiple security threats at the same time, causing major disruptions and billions of dollars of damage to enterprises. A blended threat combines different types of malicious code to exploit known security vulnerabilities. Blended threats use the characteristics of worms, viruses, and Trojans to automate attacks, spread without intervention, and attack systems from multiple points. Figure 1-3 puts things in perspective by illustrating the economics of these attacks over the past few years.

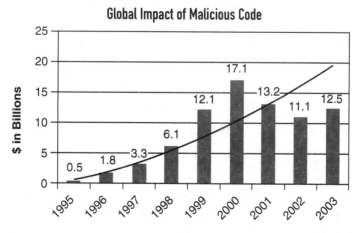

Source: *Computer Economics* 1/16/2004

Figure 1-3 Worldwide malicious code impact.

These attacks now cause losses of billions of dollars each year, so businesses can no longer ignore the problem. The Love Bug Virus in 2000 had an impact of $8.75 billion alone, causing businesses to finally recognize viruses as a significant issue and to begin to broadly implement anti-virus solutions. This work has lowered the losses experienced since that year; however, the impacts continue to be significant.

Theft of proprietary information is also a major risk to information security. When intellectual property (IP) is in an electronic form, it is much easier to steal. If this information is stored on computers connected to the Internet, thieves can potentially steal it from anywhere in the world. According to the 2003 CSI/FBI Computer Crime and Security Survey, theft of IP remains the highest reported loss. Two recent high-profile examples include an operating system product for a major software company and a version of an operating system for a major networking company. The software company theft was from an authorized third party, whereas the networking company appears to have been compromised by an unauthorized intruder. These types of security problems will only get worse as the Internet continues to grow in usage and complexity.

Three major issues have fueled the growth in security incidents: the increased number of vulnerabilities, the labor-intensive processes required to address vulnerabilities, and the complexity of attacks.

Vulnerabilities are holes or weaknesses in systems that a hacker can exploit to attack and compromise a system. For example, a system administrator can forget to limit certain restricted privileges to authorized users only. This would be like giving everyone on your street a key to the front door of your house when you only meant to give one to your family members. Other examples include existing vulnerabilities resulting from defects in computer software. In these situations, the software vendor should have identified and resolved these weaknesses during the testing processes but overlooked them while under pressure to ship new products by a deadline.

The software industry's solution to these vulnerabilities is to provide fixes in the form of software patches that a company's staff must apply to "patch" the "hole." The process of testing these patches and applying them to your environment is labor-intensive. It is often quite difficult to address the highest-level vulnerabilities and the staggering growth of new vulnerabilities compounds this problem. Vulnerabilities reported in 2003 grew by 300% from those reported in 2000. Figure 1-4 summarizes the number of CERT reported vulnerabilities over the past few years.

Growth in Security Vulnerabilities

Source: CERT

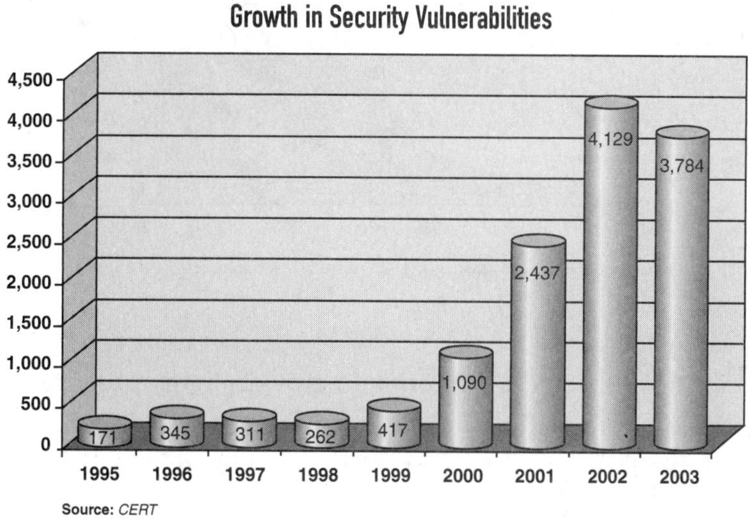

Figure 1-4 Security vulnerabilities reported.

The complexity of security attacks has greatly increased over the past few years. The early viruses caused individual productivity issues, but they had nowhere near the impact of blended threats such as Code Red or Nimda. As we mentioned earlier, blended threats use a combination of attack vectors—five in the case of Nimda—to spread more rapidly and cause more damage than a simple virus. For example, Code Red infected 350,000 computers in just 14 hours. In January 2003, the Slammer Worm hit the Internet and had an even higher infection rate than Code Red, infecting 75,000 machines in less than 10 minutes of its release.

The fastest-spreading mass-mailing worm to date was MyDoom in January 2004. At the height of the outbreak, more than 100,000 instances of the worm were intercepted per hour. MyDoom relied on people to activate it and enable it to spread. Cleverly disguised as an innocuous text file attachment, unsuspecting users opened the attachment and launched the worm.

The rapid spread of these threats makes it increasingly difficult to respond quickly enough to prevent damage. Figure 1-5 provides a look at the evolution and growing magnitude of these threats over the past few years:

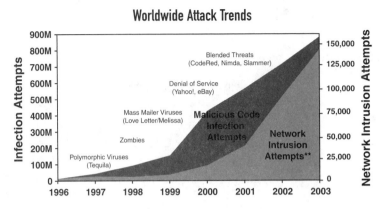

Worldwide Attack Trends

*Analysis by Symantec Security Response using data from Symantec, IDC, & ICSA; 2003 estimated
**Source: CERT

Figure 1-5   Worldwide attack trends.

The threats are expected to continue to grow in magnitude, speed, and complexity, making prevention and clean-up even more difficult. These factors contribute to the need for a proactive plan to address information security issues within every company.

Immaturity of the Information Security Market

The information security market is still in its infancy, with few formal standards established for products or services. The best way to characterize this market would be to compare it to the enterprise resource planning (ERP) market in the early 1980s. Companies at that time were purchasing finance, order processing, and manufacturing systems from separate vendors and having their IT staff integrate these products. This was a time-consuming and expensive process because no standards existed, and interoperability between different vendors was poor. The market then matured, and a small number of vendors such as SAP emerged as industry leaders. These leaders provided a complete solution for companies that included all the individual systems as part of their integrated ERP system. They also established the standards for smaller companies offering complementary functionality. Smaller companies either met the industry leader standards or were pushed out of the market.

The information security industry is at a similar stage today, with several companies offering individual solutions such as firewalls that address only a portion of a company's security needs. As a result, their customers face the challenge of making all these solutions work together. Only early versions of standards exist, forcing companies to complete multiple installations of "point" solutions that provide individual components of their security systems.

As with the ERP systems, this will change as a small number of vendors emerge as leaders and offer complete solutions that can support the majority of a company's information security needs. Smaller niche players in the market will integrate their products with these leaders' standards because their customers will no longer be willing to have their IT staff perform this role. However, until this day comes, the IT staff continues to bear the daunting task of cobbling all these solutions together. They must deploy a constantly expanding list of products and complete the integration work to ensure that these components are working together.

Another significant challenge that IT technicians face is the sheer amount of data they need to absorb to understand and manage the current state of their computing environment. Each product generates alarms, logs, and so on that they must review to determine whether something is wrong. Figure 1-6 provides a graphic overview of this situation.

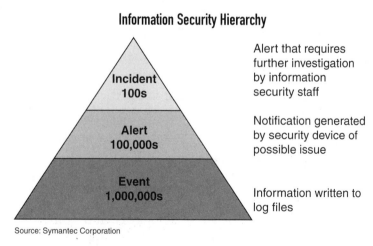

Information Security Hierarchy

Incident
100s

Alert that requires
further investigation
by information
security staff

Alert
100,000s

Notification generated
by security device of
possible issue

Event
1,000,000s

Information written to
log files

Source: Symantec Corporation

Figure 1-6 Information security hierarchy.

Security products generate a great deal of data; however, only a small number of problems or "incidents" might be affecting the company. It is difficult for security staff to get an overall picture of the security environment and put plans in place to address the critical concerns. This is similar to the business challenge in the 1990s when executive information or decision support systems were developed to *mine* through large volumes of data to determine critical business trends. Several vendors now offer decision support systems to address this issue for business executives. The "holy grail" for the information security industry is to develop similar systems to solve this problem in the security arena.

An additional challenge is the relative low priority that the software industry places on security. Although some leaders in the software industry have announced a new emphasis on security, the majority of the industry has yet to follow this example. They currently focus on making software easy to use and are under tremendous pressure to deliver new products and services, often sacrificing security. This results in the growing number of vulnerabilities. Until the software industry receives more pressure to prioritize security, even at the sacrifice of new features, this situation will continue.

It will take some time for information security vendors to offer mature solutions to protect your business. In the meantime, you must develop strategies to mitigate these risks. The good news is that the security industry is following a similar pattern to other enterprise software industries, so solutions will be forthcoming.

Shortage of Information Security Staff

Finding qualified information security staff is a difficult task, which will likely continue to be the case in the near future. Driving the hiring challenge is the immaturity of the solutions from information security vendors, the limited number of qualified staff available, and the unique blend of information security skills required. Business executives will need to invest more in this area to overcome these challenges.

Due to the immature market, lack of standards, and numerous point solutions, training is a problem for security staff. The industry has not had the time to grow the staff necessary for these roles. In addition, the information security challenges keep growing at a rapid pace, constantly expanding the list of technology to be deployed, and the information security staff just can't keep up. This translates into more time and money to get your staff trained on commercially available products.

According to the only available survey by CSOOnline.com in 2002, only 60% of the companies responding have an employee who is fully dedicated to information security, and only 32% of those individuals hold a senior-level title such as chief information security officer or chief security officer. These are relatively new titles for most, with an average of two and a half years of experience as head of information security. With the increased focus on information security, we can expect these numbers to increase in the near future.

Obtaining the necessary credentials for information security requires considerable training and experience. The Certified Information Systems Security Professionals (CISSP) credential is an internationally accredited certification and requires passing a test on a broad range of information security topics combined with a minimum of four years of work experience. The related System Security Certified Practitioner (SSCP) credential requires one year of experience plus passing an exam.

Certified Information Security Manager (CISM) also requires a minimum number of years of information security experience along with successfully passing a written exam. All these certifications require ongoing annual training as part of their certification, and GIAC requires periodic testing every two years. Security professionals holding these certifications are in high demand, and employers will need to compete to attract them to their companies. Certified Information Systems Auditor (CISA) requires a minimum of five years of work experience before sitting for an exam. SANS Global Information Assurance Certifications (GIAC) requires candidates to submit a practical work assignment as part of their certification. Certified Information Security Manager (CISM) also requires a minimum number of years of experience.

In addition to specific technical training, information security staff members need to develop security enforcement skills that are not part of the traditional IT staff background. The military, intelligence, and law enforcement fields have traditionally conducted training in this area. In some respects, a company's security policies are similar to "laws" that must be enforced within a company, which requires specialized training. This unique requirement makes it difficult for existing IT staff to transition into information security roles without receiving specialized enforcement training.

Probably the greatest challenge in this area is finding a leader who has a broad background in the field and who can pull together an effective information security team. Few candidates have been in the information security field for more than a couple of years and have the required blend of technical and security enforcement skills. They also face the leadership challenge of taking inexperienced staff and developing them into effective information security professionals while dealing with ever-increasing security risks. These individuals are rare and in high demand.

Executives will need to consider longer-term strategies to address these needs because finding trained staff is not just a question of money but also of the time necessary to build the team around a limited number of qualified staff.

Government Legislation and Industry Regulations

Recent information security incidents and increased reliance upon the Internet have prompted governments around the world to create additional legislation to regulate the technology ecosystem. This legislation spans broad areas, such as consumer privacy, to specific regulations for industries, such as health care and financial services. Because the Internet is easily accessible from many places in the world, it is important to understand and operate in compliance with these regulations. Companies that adhere to these regulations and thereby offer their customers a safe and secure method for conducting business can differentiate themselves from their competitors.

Privacy is a major issue in electronic commerce due to the high risk of misuse of personal information. Computer systems contain personal information for millions of customers, and if companies do not take the necessary precautions to ensure that this information is safe and secure, their customers can have their identities—including data such as name, address, phone number, and credit card numbers—stolen and sold to the highest bidder on the Internet. Previously, only a highly skilled hacker could break into these systems and access confidential information. This is no longer the case; now a novice can use readily available tools and gain access into these systems if the company does not use the proper safeguards.

This situation has prompted considerable legislation to protect the rights of consumers because their personal information is now much more readily available in electronic format. The European Data Protection Directive is an important regulation because Europeans take a much stricter view of privacy than the United States.

This directive prohibits the export of personal data such as name, address, and telephone number to countries that do not meet the European Union's minimum standards for consumer privacy protection. These standards require that no one can sell, rent, or transfer consumer data to a third party without that individual's explicit permission. This directive applies to customer information but also includes employee information contained in companies' internal human resource systems.

In May 2000, the Safe Harbor Agreement was enacted for U.S. companies that are regulated by the U.S. Federal Trade Commission (FTC) and have operations in the European Union. This agreement enables these organizations to comply with the European Data Protection Directive by adopting Safe Harbor Agreement Principles.

These principles require controls to ensure that personal information is protected from loss, misuse, unauthorized access, disclosure, and so on as a condition to obtain certification. Companies certified under the Safe Harbor Agreement can obtain permission to transfer data out of the European Union for renewable one-year periods. It is safe to say that other countries will adopt similar legislation for protecting the privacy of consumer information for their respective citizens.

An important consideration for business executives to remember is that laws and regulations are generally enacted on a country-by-country basis and electronic commerce is performed globally. As soon as your business uses the Internet to conduct business, you are doing business on a worldwide basis. This has the tremendous advantages of offering your products and services globally; however, you also need to comply with local regulations. These regulations are by no means consistent, and you could easily find yourself conflicting with one regulation by complying with another. The Safe Harbor Agreement is an example of the U.S. working out an agreement with the European Union to meet their regulations. Other countries will follow similar strategies to ensure that their industries are competitive and that they can operate freely in major markets such as the European Union.

One major challenge is that certain countries do not place a high priority on protection of personal information or intellectual property. They might have more pressing issues, such as food or medicine, and might be unwilling or unable to police individuals who are engaged in activities such as software piracy. These criminals operate freely in these countries without the fear of law enforcement agencies shutting down their operations. These safe havens for cyber criminals pose additional challenges for legitimate businesses that have little legal recourse to combat the illicit activities of software pirates. Unless business executives put strategies in place to protect their intellectual property and customer information, they run the risk of falling victim to these individuals.

Two industry-specific regulations in the U.S. on privacy include the Gramm-Leach-Bliley Act (GLBA) of 2001 and the Health Information Portability & Accountability Act (HIPAA) of 1996. GLBA applies to financial institutions and requires these organizations to put the controls in place to ensure the security and confidentiality of customer information. Examples of this information include names, addresses, phone numbers, bank and credit card numbers, credit history, and social security numbers. The boards of directors for these institutions are responsible for developing effective information security programs to ensure compliance with these regulations and monitoring these programs on an ongoing basis. These institutions must monitor their service providers to ensure they have the necessary controls in place to manage consumer information. Some key provisions of the act include clear disclosure of company's privacy policy regarding sharing of non-public personal information. They are also required to provide a notice to consumers and give them the opportunity to "opt out" or decline the sharing of their personal information with third parties.

HIPAA proposes to streamline the healthcare industry, reduce fraud, and make it easier for employees to switch jobs even if they have preexisting medical conditions. One of the key objectives is to standardize and automate key administrative and financial transactions that previously were paper-based. HIPAA establishes standard data formats for these transactions and the controls that must be in place to ensure that this information is secure. To ensure the privacy and confidentiality of patient's medical records, it institutes standards for the privacy of individually identifiable health information.

All companies handling medical data must adhere to HIPAA requirements for privacy—not just companies within the healthcare industry. These organizations will need to review these regulations in detail to ensure that they are in compliance.

The Sarbanes-Oxley Act is a response to the corporate corruption and failure of many companies during the Internet boom and subsequent bust that occurred during the 1999–2002 period. This U.S. law went into effect in July 2002 and is intended to protect investors by improving the accuracy of corporate disclosures. All U.S. public companies must meet financial reporting and certification mandates for all financial statements filed after June 15, 2004. Smaller companies and foreign corporations that are publicly traded in the U.S. market must meet these regulations for any statements filed after April 15, 2005.

The act is divided into 11 titles, and section 404 that addresses internal controls has generated the most concerns. The act calls for severe penalties for non-compliance, including the possibility of criminal prosecution for executives. From an information security perspective, it is difficult to achieve compliance under Sarbanes-Oxley without having an effective information security program to protect your vital financial information. Adequate controls must also be implemented to ensure that only authorized individuals are able to access this information. Change control processes must also be in place to ensure that any changes to your financial systems are implemented in a controlled manner. Finally, you need to have a business resumption program in place to ensure that your organization can continue to operate in the event of a disaster. Access and change control are covered in more detail in later chapters, whereas business resumption is beyond the scope of this book.

California Senate Bill (SB) 1386 went into effect in July 2003 and requires companies that conduct business in California to disclose any breach of security related to personal data. This law applies to both business and government agencies that own or license computerized data containing personal information. Security breaches include unauthorized access of computer data that compromises the confidentiality or integrity of personal information. Personal information includes social security numbers, driver's license numbers, and account, credit, or debit card numbers. Written or electronic notice must be given to individuals who are affected by this breach of security.

For companies doing business on the Internet, the implications of SB 1386 are far-reaching for information security because many of these businesses have customers in California and are therefore subject to SB 1386. Public notification of these security breaches can be embarrassing to companies and can have a direct impact on their brand and revenue stream. Penalties can be imposed on organizations that do not comply with the notification requirements. These regulations place additional importance on having an effective information security program in place for any company that plans to leverage the Internet to conduct business.

These are just a few examples of government and industry regulations that can affect how a company conducts business electronically. With the growing number of e-commerce security incidents, the number of regulations will continue to grow. When you start conducting business through the Internet, you are operating on a global basis and must conform to laws and regulations in many different countries. It is important to understand these laws and the restrictions that they can pose. Health care and financial services companies must give special consideration because they have specific regulations with which they must comply. Successful business executives will develop strategies that turn these challenges into competitive advantages.

Mobile Workforce and Wireless Computing

The arrival of mobile computing devices has had a significant impact on everyday life. Wireless communications liberate employees and consumers from relying on phone lines to communicate. Looking for a phone booth to make a call or going to the office to access email is quickly becoming a fading memory. Information availability and communications have greatly increased due to mobile computing devices. With the convenience of these devices, information security concerns increase because the confidential information stored on them needs to be protected.

In the past, staff members typically used one computer in the office for business purposes and a different one at home for personal use. These lines have blurred considerably over the past few years, with the use of mobile computers now surpassing the number of desktop computers that remain in a home or office. Laptop computers now enable employees to continue working at any time from any location. Personal computing devices for storing name and address information, phone numbers, and so on are no longer restricted to business professionals because teenagers now keep track of this information using mobile devices. Figure 1-7 provides some insight into current and projected usage of wireless users.

Wireless Internet Usage and Projection			
Year-End	2001	2004	2007
USA			
Internet users (millions)	149	193	236
Wireless Internet User Share	4.5%	27.9%	46.3%
Worldwide			
Internet Users (millions)	533	945	1,460
Wireless Internet User Share	16.0%	41.5%	56.8%
Asia-Pacific			
Internet Users (millions)	115	357	612
Wireless Internet User Share	34.8%	50.9%	60.4%
W. Europe			
Internet Users (millions)	126	208	290
Wireless Internet User Share	13.9%	49.6%	67.0%

Source: Computer Industry Almanac

Figure 1-7 Wireless Internet usage and projections.

The introduction of the 802.11 protocols for wireless local area networking in 1999 has revolutionized the mobile computing industry. The 802.11 protocols are the equivalent of a common "language" that enables these mobile devices to communicate with each other. Wireless adapters that take advantage of the 802.11 protocols are available for mobile devices. In some areas, wireless ISPs have begun offering high-speed Internet access without the need for phone lines or a cable connection. Accessing the Internet, sending email, and logging into the company network is now possible from the home, backyard, or your favorite park.

The challenge from a security perspective is twofold—first, all the protection offered in the company office must now be incorporated on the laptop computer or mobile device, and second, 802.11 protocols have weak security features. When physically in the office, employees can take advantage of the company's security protection such as firewalls and anti-virus software. These products can be set up to operate in the background, and employees often do not realize that these products continually protect their systems from threats such as computer viruses. When employees leave the office, this same protection must be included on notebook computers or handheld devices to ensure that they can continue to operate in a safe and secure manner. In addition to the lack of information security tools, mobile devices that might contain valuable intellectual property, customer information, or other sensitive information also run the risk of theft or loss.

New technologies often initially focus on features and functionality at the expense of security to obtain critical mass and adoption. This is the case of 802.11, as individual consumers have initially embraced this technology and are less concerned with someone reading their email or obtaining access to their personal address book. Businesses, on the other hand, cannot take those risks because enterprise systems contain vital company records that could disrupt their operations if divulged to unauthorized parties. Companies must give careful consideration before leveraging wireless technology in mainstream business.

These information security risks include all the mobile devices such as cell phones, personal digital assistants, and so on that contain valuable information. As a result, companies need to ensure that their information security program extends to all devices that frequently leave the office and that are easily lost or stolen. They can no longer count on safely locking computers in the offices when employees go home at night. Wireless communication offers many compelling advantages over traditional wired communications, but controls must be in place to ensure that the company's most valuable secrets are secure.

Information Security Challenge Summary

The Internet is a powerful tool for businesses today, and it is important to understand the inherit security risks when leveraging this technology. The Internet was based on ubiquitous communications between trusted parties that does not exist today now that the number of users has grown to hundreds of millions. Major challenges exist today that businesses must consider when leveraging the Internet, and this chapter provided some insight into the importance of including information security in your future business strategy.

These risks will not go away, and successful companies will adopt strategies to minimize them and offer unique solutions to their customers. Information security can be used as a strategic differentiator, especially in a global economy that conducts more business electronically. Secure business systems are a value-added selling tool in an increasingly savvy and cautious customer base. It is much better to incorporate some basic information security principles in your business operations rather than delegating these activities to your IT department and hoping that they adequately address them.

Essential Components for a Successful Information Security Program

The following 10 areas are essential for your information security program to be effective:

1. Make sure the CEO "owns" the information security program.

2. Assign senior-level staff with responsibility for information security.

3. Establish a cross-functional information security governance board.

4. Establish metrics to manage the program.

5. Implement an ongoing security improvement plan.

6. Conduct an independent review of the information security program.

7. Layer security at gateway, server, and client.

8. Separate your computing environment into "zones."

9. Start with basics and then improve the program.

10. Consider information security an essential investment for your business.

We will describe these components in more detail in the remaining chapters of this book and provide suggestions on how to incorporate them into your information security program.

Key Points for This Chapter

- Information security is a significant boardroom issue that executives need to understand to conduct business electronically.

- Security incidents have grown from minor annoyances to significant issues with billion dollar impacts.

- Electronic commerce has created a new channel for conducting business that relies upon an effective information security program to gain the trust of customers.

- Security incidents will continue to grow in speed, complexity, and business impact.

- The information security market is immature, and complete solutions do not exist today.

- Government and industry legislation will continue to evolve in an effort to protect consumers and enterprises that conduct more of their business electronically.

Chapter 2

Information Security Overview

During the height of the cold war, the United States had an operation, code named GAMMA GUPPY,[1] to eavesdrop on conversations between high-ranking Soviet officials while they drove around Moscow. The U.S. National Security Agency was able to intercept private conversations between Soviet Politburo members such as Premier Alexssei Kosygin, President Nikolai Podgorny, and General Secretary Leonid Brezhnev, among others, and then transmit this information back to the U.S. for processing.

During the early stages of the operation, the conversations only needed to be translated, because they did not attempt to encrypt the messages. Following a press disclosure in 1971, they began to encrypt these conversations to avoid continued leaks in this area. This did not stop the National Security Agency, which continued to intercept these messages and decode them.

An example of the confidential information that was captured included a conversation between Field Marshal Grechko and General Secretary Brezhnev that took place before the SALT I treaty was signed. Brezhnev was assured by Grechko that the heavy Soviet SS-19 missiles that they were building would fit into the lighter SS-11 launch tubes. The lighter SS-11 were allowed by the SALT I treaty, and the United States had this sensitive information during the negotiation process that occurred later.

The lack of a comprehensive information security program allowed sensitive information to be accessed by a third party, the United States government. These breaches of security continued after they were discovered, and the Soviets probably had a false sense of

1. *While there has been much retelling of Gamma Guppy, James Bamford's* The Puzzle Palace *appears to be the original source (1982, page 283).*

trust in the encryption technology they were using. This chapter reviews how to establish a comprehensive information security program that consists of people, process, and technology to protect your organization's sensitive information.

Introduction

Developing an information security program requires the right combination of people, processes, and technology solutions to ensure that your enterprise environment is secure. Your staff administers the program and develops processes to guide personnel in security-related matters. By leveraging existing technologies, you can develop a layered security strategy, also known as *defense in depth.* Understanding and evaluating these components enables you to develop an effective security program for your organization.

Overview

This chapter introduces information security principles and examines the essential components of an information security program for your enterprise. Next, it reviews the major information security technologies, introduces several information security best practices, and lays the foundation for a more in-depth review in subsequent chapters.

Enterprise Information Security Program

Three major components form the core of any information security program. Many people are involved in an enterprise information security program, and everyone plays an important role. Processes guide employees in the performance of their duties and give specific guidelines for securing your enterprise. Technology is also a key component of the program. Companies do much of their business electronically, which exposes them to additional threats. The following sections explain these components and their roles in your security program in detail.

Enterprise Security—People

Key factors to consider when creating the appropriate information security organization for your company include company size, business complexity, and the industry that you are serving. A small company operating from a few locations has very different organizational requirements from a large financial services corporation that conducts business globally.

The size of your organization usually dictates whether you create a formal information security department or combine this responsibility within another organization, such as information technology or facilities. Larger companies often have formal information security organizations that are responsible for establishing a security strategy and implementing the supporting programs.

Security staff must review and update security strategies regularly due to the dynamic nature of the information security industry. Because of this, the security personnel require regular, ongoing training to ensure that they understand new threats and can create effective prevention strategies.

Although there are no standard metrics for the ideal number of security personnel for an organization, one dedicated information security staff member for every thousand employees is common practice. The high degree of skill required of security personnel and the cost of their continuing education can reduce the cost effectiveness of using in-house staff. Many companies also prefer to focus on other core competencies. Because of these factors, they might choose to outsource all or a portion of their information security function.

Although all employees from interns to the CEO need to play an active role in ensuring the success of a security program, whenever possible, it is advisable to assign responsibility for the program to a single individual. The information security staff needs to have the support and cooperation of the executive staff to implement programs that compete with other corporate initiatives. Thus, the chief information security officer (CISO) needs to report as high up in the organization as possible, generally to the chief operating officer or chief executive officer.

Apart from the information security organization, other organizations such as legal and human resources (HR) also play key roles in the information security program because policies such as acceptable use of computers and the Internet determine the desired behavior for employees but should not conflict with labor laws.

These are some of the key considerations when developing the information security organization for your company. It is important to take a long-term view of building the organization because it can take more than one year to put an effective team in place. Having the right people in key positions is paramount to success.

Enterprise Security—Process

Well-defined policies, standards, and procedures, collectively referred to as information security processes, are the cornerstone of an effective information security program.

Policies provide the broad framework for the information security program at a given company. A security policy can restrict access to key internal systems to a small number of authorized staff. Key systems might include payroll, accounts receivable, and order processing.

Standards are the key decisions that a business has made, such as technology selection for different operations. Company standards can also define which organizations can access these systems. An example would be a company standard that dictates that all employee information is stored in the corporate human resources information system (HRIS) and that access to that data is limited to payroll and human resources staff.

Procedures are detailed, step-by-step instructions that help employees conduct their work in a safe and secure manner. For example, security processes can provide detailed procedures for someone requesting access to key systems, including forms that would need to be completed and approvals required prior to the IT staff granting access.

Key policies for an enterprise include account administration, which is the equivalent of managing which employees should receive keys to various parts of the company. It is important to ensure that employees only have access to systems that they require to perform their jobs. Allow employees access to sensitive information only on a *need-to-know* basis. In systems access context, this is referred to as the *principle of least privilege*.

For example, a human resources representative would have no reason to access restricted information about the company's merger and acquisition plans. Establishing access policies is a balancing act between enabling employees to perform their jobs efficiently and ensuring that they do so while maintaining a safe and secure environment and protecting sensitive information.

Security awareness is also important. Employees must understand their role in implementing the program and must know whom they should contact if they identify a problem. Posting policies in a very visible location such as the company intranet helps to increase understanding and adoption. Often, employees are not aware of risks, so educating them about security threats is a necessary component of an effective information security program.

Another important consideration is the ongoing nature of updating your company's security policies. The information security field is dynamic. Threats that were unlikely last year can prove to be serious next week. New threats also emerge continuously, and policies need to be dynamic to remain effective. Regular security testing procedures are required to ensure that the information security program is working properly.

Effective information security processes are a necessary component of an effective information security program. They serve as the glue between the people and technology components of your program, ensuring that they operate in a synergistic fashion.

Enterprise Security—Technology

Technology is the final and probably the most confusing element of an effective information security program. Unfortunately, much of this confusion is due to the considerable hype and exaggerated claims from the various vendors in the industry. As each promotes how its technology will address your information security needs, you might overlook one important fact—technology alone will not solve your information security problems. Some companies place too much emphasis on this area; focusing entirely upon technology can create a false sense of security and can expose your company to unnecessary risks.

From a high-level perspective, you need to evaluate the following technology components for use at your company:

- Authentication, authorization, and accounting (AAA)
- Firewalls/virtual private networks (VPN)
- Anti-virus software
- Vulnerability management
- Intrusion detection
- Content filtering
- Encryption

Refer to Figure 2-1 for an overview of how you can deploy some of these products to protect your company.

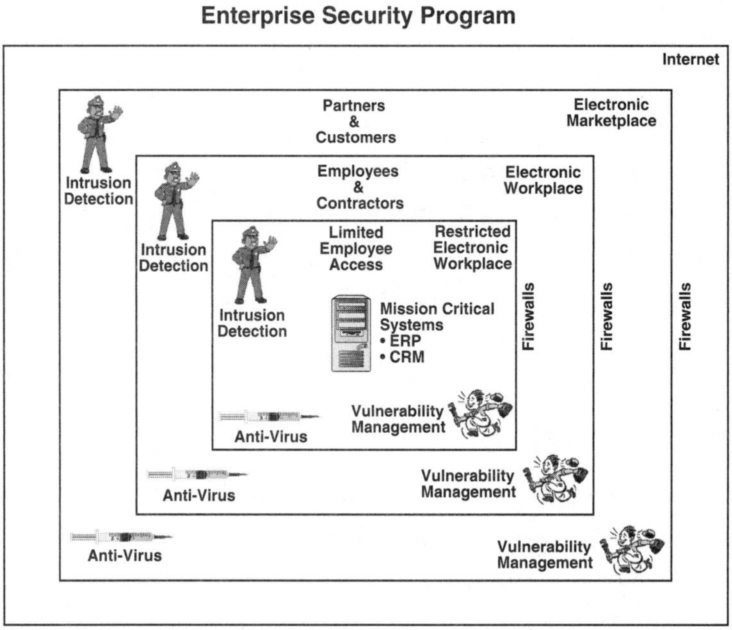

Enterprise Security Program

Figure 2-1   Enterprise security program.

It is important to note the separate zones of your enterprise security program and that many of these security products are required at each of the zones. An explanation of these zones and defense-in-depth follows.

Enterprise Defense-in-Depth

An effective architecture for any information security program involves *layering* your security to provide multiple levels of defense. This is also known as *defense-in-depth.* This includes separating your environment into multiple *digital zones* and providing protection at all the layers of your network, including the *gateway, server,* and *client* layers.

The simplest definition of a gateway is a connection or door between one section of your environment and another. A typical company has multiple connections between the Internet and the perimeter of their enterprise, and you can refer to each as a gateway.

Servers are shared computers that perform functions for multiple personnel at a company, such as storing files or running a shared application, including enterprise resource planning (ERP) or customer relationship management (CRM). Put simply, *servers* provide *services. Client* systems are composed of the individual computers that each employee uses, including PCs, laptops, desktops, and digital assistants (PDAs).

The four major zones that exist are the external (Internet), extranet, intranet, and *mission-critical zone* for your most valuable assets. Separating your computing environment into these four zones helps to isolate restricted and critical systems, such as your company's payroll, affording them a higher level of security.

The perimeter serves as the *digital gateway* around your company. *Gateway servers* reside on the perimeter of your network and separate it from the Internet. The gateway is the entry point to your network, and multiple *clients* access them.

The *intranet* is the environment where the majority of the employees conduct their work, and the *mission-critical zone* is where the most critical systems are located. Access to these systems should be tightly controlled. Refer to Figure 2-2 for an overview of these electronic zones.

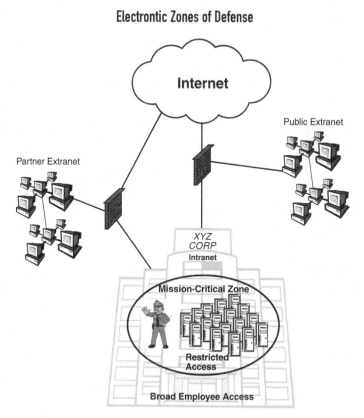

Figure 2-2 Electronic zones of defense.

The major categories of security technology include firewalls, anti-virus, intrusion detection, vulnerability management, and content management. Because threats such as viruses can cause infections at the gateways, servers, or clients, all these solutions need to be implemented at each of the three layers of your network.

Unless you provide protection at all three layers of your network, you will leave a *hole* in your environment that hackers or malicious code can compromise. This is especially true for your personal computer—when it leaves the protection of your office environment, you will need to replicate this protection.

We will now review the different security technologies in more detail and offer some guidelines on how you can use them to protect your company.

Authentication, Authorization, and Accounting (AAA)

Security issues exist when unauthorized individuals gain access to resources or when users exceed their level of legitimate access to a protected system. Information technology incorporates three tools to control access to computer systems and to restrict users to functions appropriate for their needs and authorization level: authentication, authorization, and accounting, sometimes referred to as AAA. Authentication is a process that determines who you are, authorization determines what you can access, and accounting is the tool used to audit these processes.

Everyone should be familiar with having user IDs and passwords to access computers, email accounts, and other protected systems. User IDs and passwords are the most basic form of authentication and are the equivalent of electronic keys to your information security systems. Being an essential component of your information security program, these keys need to be carefully controlled to ensure that they do not fall into the wrong hands. When a hacker obtains your keys, he can impersonate you and access your computer and network.

More advanced authentication technologies provide further security during the authentication process. These technologies include the use of physical devices or *tokens* such as smart cards that store additional information to identify a given user. Also, biometric systems can use unique biological traits, including fingerprints or retina scans, to achieve another level of authentication.

Security professionals refer to the use of two forms of authentication as *two-factor authentication.* Experts recommend two-factor authentication to control access to highly sensitive systems or for accessing systems remotely.

The traditional factors of authentication are summarized as follows:

- Something you know, such as a password
- Something that you have, such as a token
- Something that you are, such as your fingerprints with biometrics
- Where you are, such as using global positioning satellites to locate you

When employees are working from the office, it is much easier to ensure that only authorized persons are accessing your systems. For instance, you can see and identify them, and they might need to pass by a guard or use an electronic badge to access their work area.

Remote access is a special set of tools used to authenticate users when they are not physically in the office. These tools consist of software that runs on a personal computer or client and some combination of centrally located software- and hardware-based solutions that manage the authentication process.

Client software solutions include "tokens" or "certificates" that uniquely identify both the owner of the personal computer and often the personal computer itself. The software on the client and server works in tandem to make certain that the user and physical device have authorization to access a system remotely. Companies should use two-factor authentication for remote access because simple user IDs and passwords are not sufficient for keeping unauthorized personnel out.

Authorization functionality enables system administrators to restrict some special privileges to certain roles or functions that employees perform within the organization. For example, everyone at a company might have a general-use email account, but only a limited number of staff would have privileged access to add and remove email accounts. In this example, the email system contains authorization functionality and enables the email system administrator to ensure that certain restricted functions are controlled. Another example would be an accounting system that segregates duties for various members of the finance staff and only allows certain staff to access confidential information such as payroll.

Accounting is the tool that enables you to review who is accessing your systems and what they are doing. You should conduct audits regularly to ensure that no one is accessing systems without proper authorization or using them inappropriately.

For example, all staff members in a given finance area might be authorized to access the company's enterprise resource planning (ERP) system. However, if an audit indicates that employees are using the system during non-business hours without supervisors present, further investigation might be necessary to ensure these activities are appropriate.

Many companies also have multiple systems to support internal functions such as ERP, CRM, and email. Maintenance of multiple user accounts can be a time-consuming task, considering all the new hires, terminations, and responsibility changes (promotions, transfers, and so on) that occur on a day-to-day basis in large companies.

Managing user accounts across multiple systems is a daunting task, and single sign-on software is part of the industry's solution to this problem. These solutions provide a single user ID and password to access the multiple systems that can exist at a given company. Unfortunately, single sign-on software is immature, and it will take some time before solutions are working effectively across a broad range of enterprise applications.

AAA is a fundamental component of information security technology, and you can use it to determine who can access your company's systems and what functions they can perform. Security personnel must implement AAA in even the most basic information security program.

Firewalls/Virtual Private Networks (VPN)

Firewalls form the "electronic" perimeter around your computing environment. Firewalls have filters that only allow certain types of network traffic to flow into your company's network and discard any other data that does not meet preset criteria. In this way, firewalls are similar to the locks on your doors and windows—they let legitimate users and data in and keep trespassers out.

Firewall technology has tradeoffs between speed and security level. Firewalls can be categorized as follows:

- Packet filtering firewalls
- Statefull inspection firewalls
- Application layer or proxy firewalls

Packet filtering firewalls provide protection by interrogating the *header*, or address information, of a *packet*, or message, to identify potential issues, but they do not examine the *body* (commonly referred to as the "payload") of the packets. *Statefull inspection* firewalls monitor the state of a transaction to verify that the destination of an inbound packet matches the source of a previous outbound request. In other words, the firewall correlates inbound packets against previous outbound packets to determine *legitimacy*. The firewall does this correlation against a table of statefull connections and offers even more protection by examining the context of the data packets, such as the source and destination addresses of the message, rather than just filtering them. This is similar to looking at the address on a letter delivered by the mail carrier to ensure that it is addressed to someone at your company and that the return address is from someone from whom you would expect to receive mail.

The most secure firewalls, *application layer* or *proxy-based* firewalls, read and rewrite each packet to ensure that only valid messages pass through to the network. This process is more secure because it is difficult for a hacker to write inappropriate content within the data payload portion of packets. The downside is that this process sacrifices faster throughput. Several variations of these firewall solutions exist with additional levels of security at further expense to network speed.

VPN tools enable you to create a secure, private connection between two locations using a public network, such as the Internet. A VPN uses encryption to protect data so that an unauthorized third party would be unlikely to be able to read it. The secure connection, or *tunnel,* can connect an authorized individual who wants to access a remote server, such as the company email system, from a hotel room or can securely connect branch offices.

A combination of hardware and software at each location is used to establish this connection. Some firewalls also offer this capability in addition to filtering capabilities mentioned previously. VPNs are a cost-effective method of establishing a private network compared to using the traditional method of procuring a leased line, which can cost as much as several thousand dollars per month.

Firewalls provide an "electronic filter" around your enterprise and allow only authorized messages or traffic to flow into and out of your company. VPN tools enable you to establish inexpensive but secure communications between two locations.

Anti-Virus Software

Like the vaccinations that we all receive to prevent certain diseases such as polio and chicken pox, anti-virus software helps to prevent your computers from becoming infected by computer *viruses, worms,* and *Trojan horses.* Professionals refer to these electronic diseases collectively as *malware.* Hackers create hundreds of new viruses each month, which means that you have to update your anti-virus software regularly with new virus definitions to ensure that you will always have the latest cure available.

As we mentioned in Chapter 1, "The Information Security Challenge," computer viruses can spread by several methods, including email and CDs, but they require an action on the part of the user, such as opening an email attachment, to take effect. Computer worms, on the other hand, are much more dangerous because they are *self-replicating* and do not require user interaction to spread.

Attacks have gotten much more sophisticated over the years, and it is currently much easier for malware to infect your computers than it was in the past. *Blended threats* such as Nimda and Code Red (see Chapter 1) are very disruptive worms that exploit several different vulnerabilities in order to spread. These threats have prompted the security industry to develop tools that automatically push out virus definitions on a regular basis, often once per day, to protect customers. In the event that malicious code infects your computer, security vendors offer tools that remove infections from your computer and attempt to clean up any damage that the virus caused.

Anti-virus software uses two methods to protect your systems from malware: virus signatures and heuristics. Virus signatures are similar to a fingerprint; they are a reactive method because you need to know the signature in advance to detect a virus and offer protection against being infected. An example of a simple virus signature would be the words "I LOVE YOU" in the header portion of an email message because a specific virus (the "I Love You Virus") is known to manifest this behavior. A simple change made by the virus writer, resulting in what is commonly referred to as a "variant" of the virus, can change the virus signature, which requires a new virus definition to be developed. As a result, it is difficult to stay one step ahead of virus writers using only virus signatures.

Because of the dynamic nature of viruses, the anti-virus industry has developed a more proactive approach called *heuristics*. This approach looks for patterns that can identify a potential virus instead of relying on an existing database of known virus types. Heuristic features vary by vendors and range from testing the possible activities of a particular file in a *virtual sandbox* to a more extensive search of files that looks for possible combinations of codes that might identify the virus. Unfortunately, this approach is not very successful today and often creates false alarms or "false positives." Development continues in this area. Proactive protection using heuristics will become more effective over time.

Anti-virus software is a required component of your information security program due to the increasing number of viruses and frequent use of email for distribution.

Vulnerability Management

Vulnerability management is a way of proactively removing weaknesses from your information security program. An effective security program utilizes automated vulnerability management tools to identify possible vulnerabilities in your computing environment. Vulnerability management tools compare your environment against a database of known vulnerabilities to determine whether any of these vulnerabilities exist within your environment. Two types of vulnerability management tools exist: network-based and host-based. You can use network-based tools to scan network traffic to identify known vulnerabilities and host-based tools to scan physical devices such as computer servers.

Due to the increasing number of vulnerabilities, patching can represent a significant amount of work for IT personnel. Patches must be tested before being applied, and large companies can have hundred or thousands of servers and clients. Still, despite the demand on your staff, a regular program of scanning your environment for vulnerabilities and applying the necessary fixes can greatly improve your security profile.

Vulnerability management technology is an important component of your information security program. These tools enable you to proactively identify vulnerabilities and perform the necessary remediation according to your schedule, as opposed to scrambling to respond to an attack that has taken advantage of a vulnerability in your environment.

Intrusion Detection

Intrusion detection systems (IDS) monitor traffic and events on your network and clients, looking for patterns that might indicate an attack is occurring or has occurred in the past. Like vulnerability management, intrusion detection tools operate in two modes, network-based and host-based, to secure your business. Network-based tools actively scan the traffic on key portions of your network, looking for possible attacks. Network-based tools can suffer from performance issues, especially with networks becoming faster. Host-based tools operate on servers and inspect audit or log information to detect possible attacks. Because evaluating log data can be resource-intensive, these tools can negatively affect the performance of the servers they are protecting.

These tools rely upon two methods for identifying intrusions: *signature-based recognition* and *anomaly detection*. Signature-based recognition compares certain patterns of activity against known intruder attack scenarios. An example would be the *Ping-of-Death*. This attack follows a distinctive pattern of sending a large number of *Ping* commands in an attempt to overload a system. (Ping is a simple command that resembles saying "Hello. Are you there?" to a computer device and waiting for a similar response of "Yes, I am" returned back.) A signature-based IDS would recognize the pattern or signature of this attack and report it.

On the other hand, anomaly detection relies on determining patterns for normal behavior and then detecting behavior that is different from the norm. As an example, if a user or network client attempted to connect with random network hosts that it normally wouldn't contact, anomaly detection would note the divergence from normal behavior and report it.

Both of these methods face a high level of variability within any given environment between what is normal and the varying patterns an attacker might choose. As a result, intrusion detection tools can generate a large number of false positives or alarms that are unnecessary. Like the boy who cried wolf, these false alarms can undermine the enthusiasm of your staff's response when reacting to future alerts.

Intrusion detection and vulnerability management tools work in conjunction to proactively identify vulnerabilities and detect unauthorized intruders.

Content Filtering

The Internet contains a vast amount of information, the majority of which is helpful and appropriate for all audiences. On the other hand, the Internet has proven to be an effective medium for distributing inappropriate content such as pornography. Content filtering tools can filter this information, ensuring that children or your employees are not able to access it.

Two major categories of tools include web (Internet) and email filtering. You can use Internet filtering to block the viewing of certain web sites that contain inappropriate content. Internet filters often rely on databases of known web addresses or *URLs* for categories of inappropriate content such as pornography, gambling, or hate. Vendors of web filters must update the URL data-bases on a regular basis because the companies that manage inappropriate sites can be creative when trying to keep the software from blocking their sites, often changing the URL or site name. Web filters also use keywords that are considered inappropriate and block access to these sites and messages.

Spam is a huge problem today and can account for up to half or more of the email traffic at a typical company. Email filtering is similar to web filtering and can block inappropriate and unsolicited commercial email. Unfortunately, these tools are reactive today and rely on databases of known web sites or email addresses to filter content. More sophisticated tools are becoming available that also rely on heuristics to identify these messages and delete them. As with other heuristic methods, these tools are not yet fully developed, but they will continue to improve over time.

Before implementing content filtering tools, you need to consider both the legal and human resource issues. Categories such as pornography, hate, and gambling are easy to filter, but other categories such as online shopping can require much more analysis to filter. If the filtering program becomes too onerous, employees might feel you are treating them like children by censoring them or spying on them.

Content filtering is an important component of your information security due to the considerable productivity impacts of spam and employee web use (and abuse) at work. Careful consideration of legal and HR issues is necessary when establishing your content filtering strategy.

Encryption

Encryption is the process of converting data into a format that an unauthorized person cannot easily read. Two main forms of modern encryption exist: *symmetric* and *asymmetric*. With symmetric encryption, both parties use the same secret key for encrypting and decrypting messages. Asymmetric encryption is more secure, with each party having a public and private key for encrypting and decrypting.

Specifically, in asymmetric encryption, the sender of a message only has to know the recipient's public key to encrypt a message for him; the recipient then uses his private key to decrypt the message. No one can use the public key to decrypt the message or discover the private key.

Public key infrastructure (PKI) leverages asymmetric encryption and is commonly used when someone wants to communicate with another party that he does not know well. For example, if Joe wants to send a message to someone and receive delivery confirmation, he could leverage this technology. Joe would use his private key to digitally sign the message and the recipient's public key to encrypt the message; the third party could use his private key to decrypt the message and confirm that Joe actually sent the message by using Joe's public key to verify the digital signature.

The three most common areas of encryption include email (S/MIME, which uses both asymmetric and symmetric encryption), protecting critical files (usually symmetric), and Secure Sockets Layer (SSL, which uses both asymmetric and symmetric encryption) for e-commerce. In the case of email, this technology is usually hidden from the user, and options can be selected for a message to be encrypted before being sent. Newer versions of Windows offer the capability to encrypt files by utilizing the Encrypting File System. SSL is the best practice for e-commerce today. Most systems that use confidential information such as credit card numbers implement this technology.

Major Security Tool Categories

Table 2-1 provides a summary of the major information security technologies that exist today. These technologies and best practices for implementation are covered in more detail in the next chapter.

Table 2-1

Information Security Technology Overview	
Enterprise Security Technology	**Objective**
Access control (AAA)	Ensures only authorized staff, customers, vendors, or partners can access your systems.
Firewalls/VPN	Prevents unauthorized traffic from entering your network.
Anti-virus	Protects your information technology assets from malicious code.
Vulnerability management	Regular program to address possible vulnerabilities proactively.
Intrusion detection	Reacts to unauthorized access to your network.
Content filtering	Ensures that personnel do not access inappropriate material using your company's computers.
Encryption	Prevents someone from eavesdropping on your private messages, protects network traffic, and facilitates authentication.

Information Security Overview Summary

Many information security challenges exist today. It is important that you evaluate these challenges to determine which ones are relevant for your company and industry and put the necessary programs in place to protect your company.

An effective information security program using a combination of people, processes, and technology is necessary to ensure that your business is secure. We will build on these themes in the remaining chapters of the book, which describe the steps to evaluate your existing security program and how to put a strategy in place to improve the program at your company.

Key Points for This Chapter

- It is important to take a comprehensive view of your information security program, as opposed to focusing on a particular problem area.

- People, process, and technology are the essential components of an effective information security program.

- People are the most difficult portion of your program because everyone from the CEO on down needs to play his part to ensure an effective program.

- Security processes are the glue that binds the people and technology components of your program. The processes must be very clear for everyone in the organization to follow them.

- Technology is often confusing and can sometimes establish a false sense of security in your organization.

- User IDs and passwords are the most basic form of technology. Many organizations struggle with following best practices for implementing them properly.

- Technology can be deployed at multiple layers within your organization to ensure that your most valuable assets are given the highest level of protection, which is referred to as defense-in-depth.

Chapter 3
Developing Your Information Security Program

A multibillion-dollar international company found that the email of an executive based in Germany was being regularly disclosed outside the company in an unauthorized manner. The investigation was complicated. The company's corporate headquarters was in the United States, so the investigation was based there because of the extremely sensitive nature of the incident. However, the executive in question was a German citizen, the mail server used by European-based executives was in France, and the breach appeared to originate at a Dutch facility.

Who had jurisdiction? Local law enforcement in the state of California, where the company was headquartered? Federal law enforcement in the United States? The Federal Bureau of Investigation (FBI) or the Secret Service (USSS)? French law enforcement because the email server was physically located in France? German law enforcement because one of its citizens was the target? Or Dutch law enforcement because the breach appeared to originate in Holland?

What laws and regulations are investigators expected to follow? Because this issue involves personal privacy, does company policy based on United States laws prevail? Or does German law on employee privacy prevail because the target was a German citizen?

Information security can be complex and requires a consistent methodology to ensure that the program remains current with threats and changes in laws and regulations. These changes occur at a rapid pace and are not consistent across different countries and industries. This chapter reviews a methodology that can be used to develop your program and account for these changes on an ongoing basis.

Introduction

The previous chapter introduced the key components of an information security program and the principle of *defense-in-depth*. This chapter introduces the core concepts that you should consider when building a new security program or improving an existing one. Both of these tasks require a solid plan and diligent attention to details. Using the methodologies introduced in this chapter, you can begin to create that plan.

When developing your information security program, you should begin by determining the high-level business objectives that you want to achieve. These objectives will serve as boundaries for the program and will guide your progress. By following a consistent methodology, you will be able to evaluate multiple alternatives and complete the design of your program.

The concepts introduced in this chapter will continue to serve you after you have a program in place. Changing circumstances will confront you with new threats and challenges, requiring you to adjust your program over time. Revisiting these ideas will aid you when making these adjustments and continually improving your program.

Overview

Developing and maintaining an information security strategy is essential to the success of your program. This strategy serves as the roadmap for establishing your program and adapting it to future challenges. By following a consistent methodology for developing your strategy, you are more likely to achieve high-quality results during the process and complete the project in a timely manner.

In addition, it is important to communicate the strategy and the processes that your organization will follow in simple terms that your non-technical staff will understand. As Chapter 2, "Information Security Overview" mentions, the success of any security program relies on the active participation of all personnel and their compliance with established security policies. By explaining all the policies and processes clearly and with minimal technical and business jargon, you increase the likelihood that your program will succeed.

This chapter aids you in evaluating your information security program and assists you in implementing an improvement plan that is appropriate for your company. We begin with a review of a methodology that you can use to guide the process. You can complete this process in a short period—as little as 90 days for most organizations—and by doing so, you will produce a 2-year roadmap for continually improving your program. Because the information security field is rapidly changing, you should review and update this roadmap on an annual basis because major revisions might be necessary.

Information Security Methodology

The information security life cycle illustrated in Figure 3-1 offers a broad overview to managing an effective information security program.

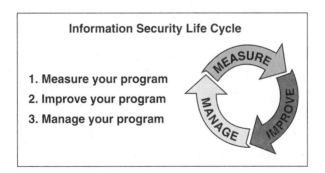

Information Security Life Cycle

1. Measure your program
2. Improve your program
3. Manage your program

Figure 3-1   The information security life cycle.

The first step is to complete a thorough review of the current state of your information security program, which is referred to as a *baseline assessment*. This review will assist you in developing the plan for improving your program in the future.

After you have completed the baseline assessment, you are in the position to begin the second step in the process—making improvements. Evaluate the risks that currently exist in your environment and develop remediation plans to address them. You will need to prioritize these risks and address them in a balanced fashion over the course of the year.

Managing your security program is the third step in the process. During normal operations and while you are making strategic improvements to your environment, you will still need to respond to tactical issues. Remember, things change on a daily basis, and you will need to continually reevaluate your priorities for improving the program.

The circular nature of Figure 3-1 corresponds to the need for repeating the process over time. The next section introduces a more detailed methodology for accomplishing this.

Formal Information Security Program

Executives commonly ask, "How well are we protected, and what should we be doing to improve our program?" A recent security-related event inside an organization or a heightened awareness of security in general can prompt this question. Regardless of the reasons for starting a formal program, you should follow a structured methodology to guide your program. Although this is true in any critical business process, it's especially important in information security. By following a structured methodology, you can obtain results that are more predictable.

A structured methodology is similar to a therapy regimen prescribed by your doctor when recovering from an illness or accident. In this case, the illness might be a non-existent or weak information security program, and an accident might equate to an information security incident.

You should first step back and determine the business objectives that you want to support with your information security program. Evaluate the effectiveness of your existing program and determine where you would like it to be in the future. Aligning your security policies closely with your business strategy enables your company to achieve its objectives without hindrance because your staff is less likely to circumvent security measures that seriously impede them from achieving your core business goals.

The next step is the *gap analysis*—comparing where you are to where you want to be and examining the alternative methods to achieving those objectives. The investment you are willing to make in your program will determine its extent and the time necessary to put it in place. Again, keep in mind that this is a continuous process and you will need to update your information security program as your business environment changes. Figure 3-2 illustrates a high-level methodology for evaluating your information security program.

Information Security Architecture Methodology

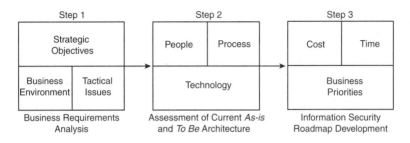

Figure 3-2   Information security architecture methodology.

Now we will examine each step in detail.

Step 1

The initial step in the process is determining the future business requirements that the information security strategy will have to support. The majority of this analysis consists of evaluating the three major areas through interviews with key managers within the company.

Strategic Objectives

- What are the company's long-term strategic goals?
- What are the major initiatives over the next 12 to 18 months?
- What are the information security requirements to meet these objectives?

Business Environment

- What is the company's line of business?
- What changes are expected in this industry over the next couple of years?
- What unique information security challenges or opportunities exist?
- How are other companies in your industry addressing information security, and which strategies have been successful?

Tactical Issues

- What information security issues currently exist that require immediate action?
- How do these issues affect the business?
- When must management address these issues?

Because it is important that your information security program supports rather than hinders your company from achieving its business goals, the results of this step necessarily form the broad boundaries for your program.

Step 2

Next, you evaluate the major components of your information security program to establish its current state and determine your goals for the program in the future. The components fall into three major categories: people, processes, and technology (the basis of your architecture). These are essential ingredients for an effective program (as we discussed in Chapter 2).

When assessing the current information security architecture, the objective is to become familiar with the existing environment, understand the current issues, and plan the future environment. This is not an exhaustive documentation of your existing environment; that level of detail is not required, and frankly, it wastes a lot of time. Some of the questions that you need to answer during this step are as follows:

- Does my organization have a formal information security strategy?
- How well has the program protected my company over the past year?
- Are metrics in place to measure the effectiveness of the program?
- Has the program undergone an independent review recently?

After establishing the current state of your program, you can begin to evaluate the possibilities for the future security environment, based upon the company's business environment and needs. The initial analysis should be broad and unconstrained because the goal is to define a long-term plan that you can tailor to what your company ultimately decides to invest in this area.

Some examples of the future environment include the following:

- A formalized organization that is responsible for information security

- Outsourcing selected portions of the program to vendors that specialize in these areas

- Upgrading your e-commerce presence to address potential security risks

- A company-wide security-awareness training program

You will use these results (that is, your gap analysis) in the final step to develop your future information security program.

Step 3

The major activities in this final step include the most important step in the process: leveraging the gap analysis between the current and future states of your program that form the foundation for the next steps required to define the roadmap. You need to develop a list of possible investment alternatives, along with the advantages and disadvantages of each one. The gaps that can exist within your program include the following:

- Your existing information security organization is not capable of managing the program

- Your company is not in compliance with industry regulations for information security

- Several high-risk areas exist within critical components of your business

Finally, you will provide the management team with alternative approaches for transforming the information security program. To make your case effectively, you must present these alternatives in business terms and specifically address how they will enable the company to accomplish the following:

- Increase revenue, improve staff productivity, and improve customer satisfaction

- Address industry compliance regarding security

- Protect company image and brand

Be clear regarding the specifics for each alternative you are proposing, how much they will cost, and how long it will take to deliver each recommended alternative. It is a good idea to circulate these alternatives within the management team during the course of your analysis, as opposed to waiting until the end to test their acceptance. Some of the changes you propose might not be readily accepted or might cost more than your company is willing to invest in information security.

Security Evaluation Framework

"How effective is our information security program?" is one of the most difficult questions to answer. Each business will judge success upon different criteria, depending on its industry and goals. A small mining company that only conducts business domestically and has few automated processes will require a different information security program from a large financial services organization that is heavily regulated and that conducts a considerable amount of business on the Internet. When evaluating these organizations, you must take into account the unique considerations of each business and industry best practices for information security.

The security evaluation framework outlined in this book includes 50 industry best practices for information security that were culled from multiple sources and presents you with a consistent methodology for grading your program. These best practices include people, processes, and technology categories. Scorecards have been developed to evaluate this component of your program. You can grade each practice area using three-tiered scoring as follows:

- "0" indicating the practice is not being followed at the company

- "1" for partial implementation of a best practice

- "2" for full implementation

The total possible score is 100 for a company that has fully implemented all 50 of the best practices. Use the results of your scores to pinpoint areas for improvement in your information security program. Identifying these areas is essential for developing your two-year improvement plan and is more important than the absolute score.

Unique company and industry characteristics are also important when evaluating your information security program because companies will vary considerably in their reliance upon security. The small mining company mentioned previously would have a low dependency upon information security, whereas security would be critical for a financial services company's operations.

The business dependency matrix (Table 3-1), which appears later in this chapter, identifies 12 critical characteristics for rating your company's dependency upon information security. By rating each characteristic as high, medium, or low importance, you can develop an understanding of how important an effective information security program is for your company.

Finally, by comparing the results of your program evaluation with your company's dependency upon information security, you can obtain a general idea of the effectiveness of your program. High-level guidelines are provided that you can use when determining the appropriate level of funding for your security program.

Conducting the Baseline Evaluation

The guidelines in this chapter offer a top-level view of the process that you should follow when evaluating your existing information security program or planning your future program. If you have not conducted an assessment in the past, you might consider bringing in an experienced third party to assist in this process. A third party will have methodologies to support evaluation and can train your staff to conduct future baselines. You should require that a third party uses industry standards rather than proprietary methodologies so that your organization can use the work it completes in the future.

Remember that this is just the first step in the process and that you need to move to your remediation step quickly to improve your security profile. Security programs can take considerable time to implement; for this reason, you should complete the evaluation as quickly as possible. You should be able to complete the methodology outlined in this book in 90 days.

Pulling It All Together

You will summarize the results of your analysis in a strategic plan that you will use as the roadmap for the next two years. Normally, one or more of the major program areas will have serious issues that you must address. It is important to start with high-level diagrams to convey your ideas and follow those with additional levels of detail. You'll find this is easier and more effective when you are presenting the plan to key individuals within the company.

You must provide management with a list of alternatives for migrating to the future information security environment along with the costs, timeframes, and benefits of each. Remember to present the recommendations in business terms and address how the program will affect revenue, staff productivity, and customer satisfaction. You'll need to test your recommendations to determine management acceptance during this timeframe.

The information security architecture document should contain the following information:

- Summary of the process used to develop the architecture

- Alternative solutions and recommendations

- Roadmap for implementation

Guidelines for developing the document include the following:

- Highly graphical

- Executive summary of 1–2 pages

- Main body of document that is 25 pages or less

- Bold recommendations because this is a great opportunity to make sweeping changes

The final information security architecture must address critical business objectives and be understandable to non-technical management. An effective approach is to find the optimal balance of addressing pressing tactical issues while also achieving the long-term strategies for the program.

Critical Success Factors

Management involvement during this process is important; management must consider information security a component of the overall business strategy for it to be effective. Otherwise, security will become just another initiative that is competing for management's attention and for limited company resources. Implementing an effective information security program will change how the company conducts business in the future, so clear communication of the process is critical. Employees need to understand these changes and the importance of information security in their organization's operations.

Another point to consider when developing your information security architecture is to set realistic expectations and not to over-commit. The costs associated with your recommendations could be significant and might require board of director approval. You must set goals that you are able to accomplish in an aggressive but achievable timeframe.

Information Security Methodology Wrap-Up

In 90 days, you can evaluate your organization's information security program and set the company on course for implementing future improvements. This requires a careful balancing act between addressing pressing tactical issues and making progress toward accomplishing strategic goals. By following a consistent methodology, you can clearly communicate to the organization the process that you will follow, get things on track, and start making visible progress.

It is important to follow a consistent methodology when establishing your information security program. The natural tendency is to look for immediate improvements when something goes wrong. However, this is a tactical rather than strategic approach, which isn't viable for establishing an effective information security program.

The methodology presented here provides an effective framework that you can easily scale according to the size and complexity of your business. The remaining portion of this chapter will cover the initial step of this methodology in more detail and provide examples of how you can use it at your company.

Business Requirements Analysis—Step 1 of 3

Follow the methodology introduced in the previous section to guide the development of your program. This includes first evaluating your unique business requirements to form the boundaries of the information security program. Major areas that you will evaluate include the strategic objectives for your program, your company's business environment, and tactical issues that you need to address immediately.

As we have emphasized, people, processes, and technology are the major components of an information security program. It is important that you carefully balance these areas because it is easy to focus on a single area such as technology and overlook other important components. Company size and complexity, risks, and unique business factors will define your individual program. A pragmatic approach to evaluating each area is outlined in the following sections.

Strategic Objectives

You can only establish specific security goals after you have clearly articulated strategic business objectives. You need to understand the real security risks and vulnerabilities that your business faces every day. Executives need to work together with the leader of their information security program to establish the company's long-term security objectives. This approach forces the company to think about security at an appropriately high conceptual level.

One example of a strategic objective for your information security program would be the appropriate handling of customer information. Companies now conduct much more business electronically, and their customers trust them with their confidential information. Unless the necessary controls are in place to secure this information, it is possible for dishonest individuals to steal personal information such as credit card numbers and make unauthorized purchases.

Balancing time to market and security is another objective for companies to consider for their information security program. Businesses today are under tremendous pressure to offer new products and services, and how they handle security issues that arise is a major issue. In particular, software companies must decide between shipping a new version of their software sooner even though it contains security bugs or delaying the ship date to address these defects. Shipping sooner can have a direct bearing upon the projected revenue from the new product, but failing to address bugs can negatively affect the company's brand image if something goes wrong.

Ongoing involvement of the executive staff is an important consideration for your information security program. Having active involvement of the executive staff can improve the likelihood of the program's success, but this will divert some time and attention from other activities. Depending too little on the executive staff can result in them pushing the program too far down in the organization. This will have the opposite effect and set up the program to fail.

The level of investment is another important consideration because many programs need to compete for limited resources within a given company. If your company considers information security of strategic importance, it must allocate the necessary funds to ensure that the program is successful. If the company decides that information security is a core competency, it must spend the necessary time and money to build an in-house team. On the other hand, it might be more appropriate to rely upon expert third parties to provide this service.

As you continue to add and improve security, keep in mind that 100 percent security is not a realistic goal. The pervasiveness of security threats, the broad diversity of enterprise networks, and the ingenuity of hackers contribute to this fact. Successful security is more about ceaselessly implementing incremental measures that reduce overall risk. Of course, you must always balance security against other business needs of the enterprise.

The following are examples of broad objectives that your company might develop.

Information Security Guiding Principles

1. We will use comprehensive architectural planning to ensure that all elements of the information security program are defined and planned.

2. We will design information security solutions for global operations from the outset, rather than local solutions that are enhanced for "international idiosyncrasies."

3. The executive staff owns information security, and it is responsible for approval of policies and oversight of the program.

4. We will treat our customer's data with the highest level of confidentiality and not share this information with third parties without customer permission.

5. We will not implement a new system that will harm our customers by disclosing their confidential information to unauthorized parties.

6. We will comply with all industry and governmental security regulations 30 days prior to required deadlines.

7. We will carefully balance the business need to quickly offer new products and services against the security risks it might pose to our customers or damage to our company brand.

8. We will adopt proven leading-edge information security technologies that will protect our company and customers.

9. We will identify internal information security core competencies to address essential value-added activities and outsource all other information security activities.

10. We will invest in information security at or above industry benchmarks for our business.

Upon completion of your strategic objectives, you are in a position to leverage this work when developing your future information security program and guiding the daily operation of the program. Your objectives should not change dramatically over time, and you should evaluate key decisions and align them with the overall goals of the program.

Business Environment

Every company has a set of unique criteria that determines how it conducts business, and your information security program should support your company's business environment. Company size, complexity, and industry are a few of the criteria that you need to consider when developing your program.

Scale your information security program to the size of your company. A smaller company, where the staff performs multiple functions, might not have a formal information security department or a CISO. In fact, a single individual might perform all the information technology and information security functions of the company.

On the other hand, a larger company that does a significant portion of its business electronically might need to have a CISO. Because disruptions to online systems can have significant impacts to the business, a more formal information security organization can prove to be an advantage.

You also need to scale security processes to the size and complexity of your organization. A smaller company might be able to operate effectively with a few informal policies. When companies expand into multiple offices and geographies, the need for formal policies becomes much more important.

Finally, the industry that your company is serving can determine the importance and scope of your information security program. Financial services industries require higher security due to the potential effect that fraud can have on their business. The health care industry also has high standards for security. Federal regulations require that health care providers protect sensitive personal medical information. In contrast, many small businesses that do not rely heavily on computer systems will not require an extensive information security program.

Table 3-1 provides some criteria that you can use to determine the importance of information security at your company. Using a simple method of 3 for high, 2 for medium, and 1 for low, you can grade your company's dependency upon information security. Note: These forms are provided in Appendix A, "Security Evaluation Framework," which you can photocopy and use at your organization.

Table 3-1

Information Security Business Dependency Matrix	
Component	**Ratings** **(High - 3, Medium - 2, Low - 1)**
Company Characteristics	
■ Dependence upon systems to offer products and services to customers	
■ Value of company's intellectual property stored in electronic form	
■ Requirement for 24-7 business systems	
■ Degree of change within company (expansions, M&A, new markets)	
■ Business size (number of offices, number of customers, level of revenue) and complexity (processes, systems, products)	
Industry Characteristics	
■ Budget for security administration and security initiatives	
■ Potential impact to national or critical infrastructure	
■ Customer sensitivity to security and privacy	
■ Level of industry regulation regarding security (GLBA, HIPAA)	
■ Brand or revenue impact of security incident	
■ Extent of business operations dependent upon third parties (partners, suppliers)	.
■ Customers' ability to quickly switch vendors based upon their ability to offer services in a secure manner	
Average Overall Ranking (Total Scores/12)	

By using this simple ranking, you can obtain a general idea of your company's dependence upon information security. Because no two companies are the same, you can modify this table to evaluate your entire business or to examine specific parts. If you find that your company is highly dependent upon information security, the remaining portions of this book contain detailed suggestions for a comprehensive review and improvement of your program.

If your company has a low ranking, you might want to be more selective in your review and improvement plans because you might not want to devote many resources to security at this point. However, you will want to revisit this analysis on a periodic basis as your company expands and offers new products and services. Your business might become more reliant upon information systems and might need an information security program in place to protect these systems in the future.

Tactical Issues

Although it is important to take a long-term view of your information security program and develop a solid strategy, you might need to address some immediate issues. This can include tactical issues that your company is facing due to either industry requirements or government regulations. As we have mentioned, the health care and financial services industries have some specific requirements that they need to address to conduct business.

On the other hand, you might have recently been hacked and might need to address customer concerns regarding your handling of confidential information. Of course, this takes precedence over all other activities. Regardless of the nature of the issue, you need to do something before you are able to complete your future strategy.

Developing a *90-day tactical plan* is an effective way of addressing these issues while you're completing your strategy. Ninety days is enough time to complete the analysis necessary to develop your information security strategy and to begin remediation of any tactical issues. At this point, you should resist the natural urge to go completely into tactical mode. Address some of the most serious issues; however; you need to balance this against the strategic goals for the organization.

Key objectives for the 90-day tactical plan include the following:

- High-visibility issues that need to be addressed now
- Critical decisions that cannot be postponed

- Quick wins that can be accomplished, garnering support for the information security program

- Defer major architectural decisions and large expenditures until the overall information security strategy has been developed

The plan sends a message to your organization that you are aware of the key issues and have plans to address them now. It also provides an opportunity to improve the rapport with members of the organization who might not be pleased with your current information security organization while showing that you can make a difference.

In the initial discussions about the information security program, it is important to understand the business strategy, along with existing pain points. Look for *quick wins* that you can accomplish during the first 90 days that will help you win support for strategic initiatives that will be more difficult to accomplish. It is also important to identify or create *business champions* of the new information security initiatives. The enthusiasm of these early supporters will drive the funding and implementation process.

During the first 90 days, it is important to *over-communicate* whenever possible, including both good and bad news. Spend a great deal of time with the key managers and the information security staff to understand the situation before drawing any conclusions. One technique that can be effective is to develop a consistent status report to communicate the progress during the first 90 days. Monitor critical information such as the project objectives, recent results, and upcoming milestones and address progress on key issues that management has identified. By following this approach, you can communicate using a common methodology and minimize any misunderstandings regarding the information security program.

Your 90-day plan will be successful if you can accomplish the following:

- Address some of the current pain points in the organization

- Establish a rapport with key organizations that are affected by this program

- Set up a consistent mechanism for tracking the status of projects
- Avoid the urge to make major architectural decisions until you have conducted adequate research

Remember, no two companies are the same, and you will need to customize your tactical activities, just as you did with your strategic activities. The key point is to make an immediate improvement to the organization while you are developing your strategic plan. The organization will probably not remember what occurred during the 90-day period but rather that you addressed some key issues and developed a strategy.

Business Requirements Summary

The result of this analysis needs to be a broad range of strategies that you can use to develop some achievable objectives for the next few years. These objectives must be broad enough to guide the information security program and provide the organization with a specific roadmap for implementation. For example, a company in the health care industry might have a broad objective of staying in compliance with HIPPA regulations and offering online access to critical medical information to their customers within the next six months. This is an example of broad boundaries that will help to guide deliverables for the information security program.

Objectives will vary considerably between companies and will serve as the overriding principles for an information security program. Company size, complexity, and line of business are a few examples of criteria that will drive the appropriate information security program for your business. Compare any activity that you pursue to these objectives to ensure that you are in alignment. Always tailor your information security program to meet your company's requirements; doing the opposite is the surest route to failure.

After completing your business requirements analysis, you are in a position to proceed with the second step of the methodology, which evaluates your current information security program and designs your future desired program. This step is divided into the three key program components: people, processes, and technology. The next three chapters address each component in turn.

Developing Your Information Security Program Summary

This chapter introduced the information security life cycle and reviewed a methodology that can be used to develop an information security program for your organization in approximately 90 days. The methodology begins with establishing the current state of your program, commonly called your "baseline," and provides the steps required to develop a plan to reach your desired future state. We followed the first step of the methodology and reviewed the steps necessary to complete the business requirements analysis portion of your information security program.

Key Points for This Chapter

- A structured methodology should be used when developing your information security program.

- The first step in this process is to determine the business objectives that you want to accomplish with your program, such as providing the highest protection possible for your customer's sensitive information.

- Assessing the current state of your program and determining the desired future state is the second step in the process.

- The final step includes gap analysis between your existing program and desired future program and providing alternatives to bridge this gap.

- The Security Evaluation Framework is a tool that can be used to guide this process and develop an information security roadmap in 90 days.

- The framework includes the ability to tailor your program based upon unique company and industry characteristics because no two companies are the same.

Chapter 4

People

The CEO of a multibillion-dollar wireless company had just finished his presentation to the Society of American Business Editors and Writers in Irvine, California, only to discover that his laptop was missing. The laptop contained highly sensitive company information, and the CEO was quite concerned that it would be of great value to "foreign governments." The company had been in conversations with Chinese telecom carriers and was hopeful they would adopt their patented technology.

The laptop was never recovered, and it is hard to determine whether a foreign government could have used this information because they would have had to pay royalties for patented technology. However, the incident does highlight a potential issue for senior-level staff who routinely carry sensitive information on electronic devices such as laptops and PDAs. This chapter covers the people portion of your information security program, which will be the most challenging aspect of setting up your program because everyone in the organization needs to play his part to ensure success.

Introduction

The importance of information security has prompted many consultants to update their business cards without really investing much in this developing field. Some qualified experts do exist in this industry, but few consultants truly understand it *and* have proven experience to back up their claims.

Considerable information exists about best practices for information security; however, the real test is to have these practices implemented at your company. Day-to-day management of your information security program is where the "rubber hits the road," and getting everything to operate smoothly can be difficult. Successful organizations will leverage outside help and construct a program that is effective for ensuring their company's security.

Overview

People are the most important component of an effective information security program, and this chapter begins with a critical evaluation of this component within your existing organization.

The previous chapter introduced the security evaluation framework, which contains some of the most important industry best practices for information security. The first step is using it to grade your existing program and identifying potential areas for improvement. The design of your future information security organization is the second step in this process.

This chapter divides the current and future people evaluation into three key areas that correspond to the security evaluation framework: strategy, components, and administration.

People—Strategy

The existence of a comprehensive information security strategy demonstrates that your information security organization is planning to migrate from your existing program to your company's desired future program. Your information security organization must update the strategy regularly because new information security challenges arise daily. If your staff is scrambling to react to new threats, it probably isn't prepared, and its strategy probably reflects this deficiency.

You can also review how well the organization has put the necessary controls in place to protect the company over the past year. The number of security incidents occurring over the past year and the severity of the impact upon your business are ways of quantifying the effectiveness of your program.

Determine whether the organization has addressed key *information security compliance* issues for your industry. Depending on your industry, you might have to comply with a number of regulations, such as HIPAA for the health care industry. You cannot ignore these issues, and the ability of your information security staff to prepare your organization is quite important and a good reflection of its capabilities.

Achievement of industry-recognized certifications, such as British Standard (BS) 7799, is another indication that your security organization has addressed the best practices for information security. BS 7799 certification has stringent requirements for documenting your information security practices and requires a considerable investment of time and money.

People—Components

It's necessary to evaluate the information security organization and determine whether personnel have the skills and credentials they need to ensure the program's success. Consider the following questions:

- Who is responsible for information security at your company today?
- Are they part of a formal information security organization, or do they work in another department?

Having a dedicated information security organization in place is a positive indication of an effective information security program. Dedicated security staff with a clear reporting path are better suited to managing and implementing your security program.

When evaluating your staff, evaluate the qualifications and experience of the organization's leader and group members with the following questions:

- Are they certified information security professionals with credentials, such as Certified Information Systems Security Professional (CISSP), that are accepted by the industry?
- How effective is the leader of this organization, and is he capable of supporting the future needs of the company?

The information security industry changes on a regular basis, so it is important to have someone leading your organization who can adapt to the increasing security challenges you will be facing.

People—Administration

Well-defined roles and responsibilities are important for any organization to be successful within a corporation, and information security is no different. Does the leader of your information security program have sufficient authority to put security policies in place and enforce them throughout your company? If your staff has responsibility for information security but little or no authority to enforce the program, it is unlikely to succeed.

The support of the executive staff is critical to gain the necessary commitment of all organizations to the information security program. Management must be aware of the challenges of the information security program and the progress that is being made. Regular reporting to the executive staff and board of directors ensures that the program receives appropriate oversight.

Segregation of duties is another area to consider in your people evaluation. For example, good financial controls suggest segregating staff responsible for setting up a vendor from those who can authorize a payment. You should also separate groups responsible for day-to-day security operations from those responsible for auditing your security program. For example, at a major computer manufacturer in Silicon Valley, a husband who worked in the finance organization and his wife who worked in the information technology department colluded on return merchandise authorizations to defraud the company of several hundred thousand dollars. In this example, the wife should not have had privileged access to the same systems that her husband used legitimately for his day-to-day work. Both employees were convicted and sentenced to jail.

Obtaining the support and involvement of key organizations in your company is also essential for success. Have organizations such as legal and human resources participated in the establishment and management of the information security program? Key components of the information security program can place restrictions on employee's behavior, so these organizations need to be actively involved to ensure that employee relations issues are considered and that employees are aware of the penalties for noncompliance. It is also important to recognize the global aspects of your information security program because it will need to address the entire organization, not just the staff located in a particular location such as your headquarters.

Your information security organization also should actively manage risk. Your staff members' level of involvement in determining whether new products and services have potential security risks indicates how well they have aligned themselves with your mainstream business goals. The degree to which they evaluate information security compliance with existing products and services is another area to consider. On a periodic basis, they should review incremental changes to products and service offerings such as storing customer information on your e-commerce site.

These are only a few of the questions that you can use to determine the ability of the existing organization to support your future information security needs. It's important to take an objective view of this area to determine whether your existing organization is capable of running the information security program. You also need to recognize that people are the most critical component of your program and that no amount of sophisticated technology is going to solve the information security challenge alone.

Table 4-1 is a scorecard that you can use to grade your information security organization. The scorecard uses a simple "0–2" scoring method to indicate the compliance in each area, with "0" signifying that this practice is not being followed, "1" for partial implementation, and "2" being the highest score for full implementation.

Table 4-1

Information Security People Evaluation		
Component	**Score(0–2)**	**Comments**
Strategy		
■ Written information security strategy		
■ Strategy updated on a regular basis		
■ Proactive versus reactive organization		
■ Minimal impacts to business operations due to security issues		
■ Industry compliance issues (for example, HIPAA) have been addressed		
■ Industry certifications (for example, BS 7799) have been achieved		
Components		
■ Qualified leader (for example, CISSP) of organization		
■ Experienced staff with necessary training		
■ Dedicated information security staff		
■ One staff member per 1,000 personnel		
■ Ongoing training program in place		
Administration		
■ Function provides regular status reports to executive staff and board of directors		
■ Executive staff owns the information security program		
■ Active engagement with critical functions such as human resources and legal		
■ Authority to enforce information security program		
■ Segregation of duties		
■ Performs risk analysis and management (assessments, audits, and compliance)		
Total Score (0–34)		

This is by no means a comprehensive list of questions. However, it does give you an idea of which key areas of your existing information security organization you will need to evaluate.

Having the right organization in place is paramount to your overall information security program. Without an effective organization, your investments in other areas such as security technology are worthless. You should use the results of this evaluation to determine the effectiveness of your existing organization and to identify potential areas of improvements.

A grade of 25 or less indicates significant deficiencies in your existing program. You will use the results of this evaluation later in your analysis when you design your future information security organization.

Design of Your Future Organization

Now that you have developed a baseline of your existing organization, you are in a better position to plan for the future. You will use the information security framework and the same categories of strategy, components, and administration to drive the design process.

People Strategy

For any security program to be successful, designated people must be trained in and held accountable for security. It's time to step back and take a holistic view of your security organization. Working from your baseline assessment, you should focus on hiring and organizing your personnel. Assembling your security "dream team" can take as little as six months or more than a year, but you can begin building the framework for it today.

This section highlights some of the key decisions that you will need to make about your information security organization. Although solving the issue of people is the most challenging, having the right staff can easily make up for deficiencies in processes or technology.

Key People Decisions

You can summarize decisions regarding your information security staffing into two major categories: building an in-house capability versus reliance upon a third party, and making a series of structural choices for the organization. When evaluating these decisions, consider the following questions:

In-house information security staff versus use of a third party such as managed security services

- Is information security a core competency that you want to develop within your organization?
- Do you prefer to rely upon a third party for all or some portion of your program?
- Do you have a short-term need for a third party who will help improve your program and then transfer its knowledge to your staff?
- Do you have a qualified leader of the organization?
- Does your staff have adequate training, and do they hold industry-recognized credentials (for example, CISSP)?
- Are you willing to put an ongoing training program in place to ensure that the staff achieves industry-recognized credentials?

Information security organization structural choices

- Do you want to follow a centralized versus decentralized organization structure?
- How do you want to segregate the responsibilities within the organization?
- What are the roles and responsibilities of the information security staff?
- What is the optimal mix of staff within the information security organization?
- How do you want to structure a governance board for information security at your company?

In-House Versus Outsourcing

Finding trained staff is not easy, so you might want to rely on third parties to perform some of your information security functions. Outsourcing eliminates tedious work and enables your staff to concentrate on important tasks such as defining processes, implementing them properly, and making sure that they fit into your environment.

To establish a staffing strategy, you need to identify the core information security competencies that you want to retain in-house. Do you consider information security a core competency for your organization, and are you willing to invest the necessary time and money to develop this function at your company? It's not possible to excel in all areas of your business, and you should consider hiring third parties to perform functions outside of your organization's core competencies. Some areas that you might consider outsourcing are these:

- Evaluation of security log information. Security devices generate a large amount of data, and reviewing this data is time-consuming, tedious, and clearly not the best use of your security staff's time.

- 24-7 monitoring of your information security systems.

- Auditing and compliance.

- Initial setup of portions of your program, such as installing firewalls and training your existing staff.

You need to ensure that someone within your company is responsible for managing the vendor relationship. That individual needs to supervise in-house and third-party staff to ensure that your information security program is successful. This position should be a senior-level individual who must establish clear expectations with the vendor and conduct periodic performance reviews to ensure that the vendor meets your service levels.

Knowledge transfer is a key concern whenever you use a third party to address some area of your program. You need to make sure that a third party transfers its knowledge to your internal staff, or else you will continue to rely on this vendor for a much longer time than you expected. Include knowledge transfer in the contract; most vendors don't offer this up front.

Should you decide to outsource some portion of your information security program, following are some key selection criteria:

- Proven solution to your information security problem backed up by actual customers who are willing to provide detailed references

- Reputable company with financial resources to continue on long-term basis

- Ability to provide high level of service 24 hours a day and 7 days a week

- Willingness to conduct "proof of concept" pilot to ensure that product or service addresses your business problem

- Long-term strategy to deliver future information security solutions to their customers

Outsourcing is a critical area that you should evaluate on a regular basis to ensure that you are providing the most effective security solutions for your organization.

Industry Regulation Compliance

Preparing your company for compliance with industry regulations is a complex process that is subject to frequent change due to the shifting regulatory landscape. Keeping this in mind, this section presents some of the key areas that you should consider and some general best practices for compliance. Details for compliance with specific regulations are beyond the scope of this book and might require that you consult professionals with expertise in this area.

Due to the dynamic nature of this area, it is important to identify current and pending regulations that exist for your industry. Considerable information is available on the Internet, and a list of helpful web sites is provided in Appendix B, "Information Security Web Sites." Some current key regulations include the following:

- GLBA for the financial services industry, also known as the Financial Services Modernization Act of 1999

- European Union (EU) Data Protection Directive for handling of personal information

- Safe Harbor for U.S. companies to comply with the EU Directive

- HIPAA for the health care industry

- CA 1386 for all companies that conduct business in California

- Sarbanes-Oxley for all companies publicly traded in the United States

The majority of this legislation regulates protecting data, especially personal information, from inappropriate use. From a best practices perspective, your information security program needs to achieve the following objectives:

- Ensure the confidentiality of personal information.
- Protect personal information from any integrity issues from unauthorized modifications.
- Ensure personal information is available when you need it.

Protecting your data is the fundamental objective of your information security program. Practices for realizing this objective include requiring passwords and other forms of authentication for accessing sensitive data and encrypting personal information to prevent unauthorized parties from reading it. All the people, process, and technology components of your program must address your information security needs based upon business criticality and regulatory compliance.

People—Components

At some point, you might decide to create a formal information security organization. A dedicated information security organization has the inherent advantage of focusing individuals on specific areas, such as managing a security awareness program or monitoring program compliance. Having the right team in place can make all the difference in your program's success.

Hiring and Developing Your Team

Information security professionals are in high demand today. If you decide to develop an in-house information security organization, you need to be willing to invest the time and money necessary to attract, develop, and retain these employees. If you aren't willing or are unable to make the necessary investment at this time, you might be better off outsourcing some or all of your information security functions.

As we have mentioned, having the right team in place can easily be the single most important element of an effective information security program. Broadly speaking, information security personnel fall into three major categories:

- Management
- Technical
- Audit staff

Ideally, you want to hire individuals who have a blend of technical and business skills. The technical background is necessary to understand complex computing infrastructures and the various alternatives for protecting them. Business experience is necessary to offer security alternatives that fit your company's operations and explain them in terms that your executive staff will comprehend.

Security Management

The leader of your information security program needs to have a broad understanding of both information security and your business operations. In addition to experience in leading this function at comparable companies, you should look for some of the previously mentioned credentials. An information security manager should have either a Certified Information Systems Security Professional (CISSP) or Certified Information Security Manager (CISM) certification because these represent a broad understanding of information security essentials.

Technical Staff

In addition to management, you need staff members who can conduct the daily operations of your security program. These personnel must have the appropriate technological skills for their area of security and, ideally, some level of business knowledge. Depending upon the size of your organization, you might have team members who focus on a single technology such as firewalls or broader areas such as all UNIX-based systems.

The best certifications to look for among your technical personnel are the SysAdmin, Audit, and Network Security (SANS) technical certifications. These are well-recognized and vendor-neutral, and they have the buy-in of other organizations within the information security community. Avoid vendor-specific certification programs because they are narrowly focused, and few of them address information security well.

Security Auditing

Security audit personnel are necessary to ensure that your program is operating in compliance with your established policies. The information security policy cycle consists of establishing information security policies, day-to-day implementation, and back-end compliance. Your security audit staff plays a key role in ensuring that you establish appropriate policies and later that your organization remains in compliance with them.

Staff members in these roles need to have a good understanding of information security programs, previous audit experience, and (ideally) Certified Information Systems Auditor (CISA) credentials. Personnel in these roles not only measure compliance with information security policies but also provide alternative solutions to remedy compliance issues.

What Credentials to Look For

When reviewing the credentials of potential employees, a few different acronyms might appear after their names, indicating that they hold one or more industry certifications. These certifications are important because they indicate that the individual has security-specific knowledge and work experience. Some of the most prestigious security certifications are described here.

Certified Information Systems Security Professionals (CISSP)

CISSP is the worldwide gold standard in certification for senior information security managers in business and government service. CISSP certification attests that the holder has detailed knowledge of the 10 *security domains* in the *Common Body of Knowledge,* as designated by the International Information Systems Security Certifications Consortium, Inc. (ISC)[2] To receive CISSP certification, individuals must pass a written exam administered by the ISC[2] and have a minimum of five years of work experience in one or more of the 10 domains.

Certified Information Security Manager (CISM)

CISM is a new (2003) certification from the Information Systems Audit and Control Association (ISACA). The ISACA designed the CISM certification to be business-oriented and focused on information risk management while at the same time addressing security management, design, and technical issues at the conceptual level.

CISM is for the individual who must maintain a view of the "big picture" by managing, designing, overseeing, and assessing an enterprise's information security. It is a good credential for someone in a security management position. A CISM credential requires successful completion of the CISM exam and a minimum of five years of information security experience, including three years in a management role. Ongoing information security education is also a requirement for CISMs.

Certified Information Systems Auditor (CISA)

CISA certification is another globally recognized symbol of achievement, with a focus on a different area of security from a CISSP. CISA applicants must have a minimum of five years of professional information systems auditing, control, or security work experience under their belt before they can take the CISA exam and must follow up with continuing education courses each year. A CISA's special areas of knowledge are IT compliance and auditing.

SANS Global Information Assurance Certifications (GIAC)

Ideally, employees who are involved with day-to-day security operation of your enterprise will have GIAC certification. The SANS Institute founded *Global Information Assurance Certification* (GIAC) in 1999 in response to the need to validate the skills of security professionals.

GIAC is the only certification that requires candidates to submit a practical assignment to demonstrate real-world, hands-on mastery of security skills. In addition, GIAC-certified employees must renew their certification regularly so that certificate holders remain current on the latest threats, technology, and security best practices.

Certification Programs

In the late 1980s and early 1990s, many certified professionals had little, if any, practical work experience. As a result, many IT certifications became almost worthless as an indicator of technical expertise. They only established that an individual could study for and pass a multiple-choice test. This is still a problem with many vendor-specific certifications.

The previously mentioned security certification programs avoided this problem by requiring applicants to have quantifiable (and verifiable) work experience in information security. One of them, the SANS, requires certified persons to revalidate and retest every two years. The ISC and ISACA certifications require continual professional development. ISC- and ISACA-certified persons must submit documentation each year demonstrating that they are continuing their security training and remaining current with the changing technology.

Employee Training

Information security is never stagnant, and your employees' professional development shouldn't be either. Encourage them to participate in security training to keep them up-to-date. This might include paying for training, certification, or conference attendance or bringing third-party security educators to your workplace.

Some of your staff members might assume information security roles without specific training or experience in this area. Obtaining the previously mentioned security certifications is a good goal for your training program. While working toward certification, your less experienced staff members acquire information security principles that they will incorporate into their daily work activities.

Optimal Staff Mix

After you have determined the skills required within the organization, you need to determine the appropriate mix of staff. Employees who have good work experience, backed up by industry-recognized credentials, will make all the difference when building an effective information security staff. Generally, you will need one manager and one security audit professional, with the remaining personnel filling the operational roles.

You can organize technical staff by security technology or business geography. Depending upon the size of your organization and the geographic dispersion of your company, you might need to have staff members assume multiple roles. If this is the case, ensure that your team has the necessary skills to fill these broad responsibilities.

Focus on quality, not quantity, when building your information security team. When you have an effective information security team in place, you can leverage other parts of the organization around a small core of qualified staff, delegating many of the day-to-day operations of your program to your IT organization.

The Staffing Challenge

As we have said, finding skilled, experienced security professionals can be difficult. The disparity that exists today between the supply and demand of skilled information security professionals is among the largest in IT. Unfortunately, you might not be able to fill your security openings in a reasonable period of time. Often the search for the right candidate can take more than a year.

Consider turning to recruiters who specialize in information security employment. Often this will work better than attempting to locate and hire staff on your own. A good specialized recruiter will have many contacts throughout the information security community and should be capable of coming up with a number of good candidates for you.

At this point, it's worth mentioning a long-standing debate in the information security community—whether to hire so-called *black hats* and *gray hats*. Black hats are individuals who have gained their security skills unethically, even by breaking the law. Hiring a black hat for your information security team is analogous to hiring a burglar to watch your offices. It's not an acceptable practice, and businesses shouldn't hire these individuals, reformed or not.

Gray hats are individuals who claim to be reputable security consultants yet who enjoy looking for security vulnerabilities in various types of products. During their explorations, gray hats often walk a fine line between legal and illegal behavior. The security community continues to debate the practice of hiring gray hats, but it should not be as great a concern as hiring black hats. As with any employee, conduct thorough preemployment screening, including a background check.

Bad Guys

To establish an effective information security program, you need to have an understanding of individuals who are commonly referred to as *hackers* that pose risks to the smooth operation of your business operations. Hackers range from bored students to cyber terrorists. In the past, hackers possessed a high level of technical knowledge. Nowadays, it isn't necessary to be a computer expert to become a hacker because thousands of web sites offer automated hacking tools. Table 4-2 presents a broad overview of the demographics of the hacker community.

Table 4-2

Changing Attacker Demographics			
Classification	**Attacker Description**	**Target**	**Results**
Computer crime	Vandal, Script Kiddie, Packet Monkey	Email, Web sites	Downtime, defacement, denial of service
Computer crime	"Criminal Hacker," "Black Hat"	Assets	Monetary gain
Information warfare	Government organization	Political infrastructure	Political power, balance change
Cyber terrorist	Terrorists, nonstate actors	Physical infrastructure	Destruction

Source: Symantec

Your information security organization must understand the hacker community to protect your company's critical assets because it will be facing hackers on a daily basis. Hackers are good at preserving their anonymity; they often use aliases and usually remove traces of their attacks.

Hackers share information and tools over the Internet using newsgroups and web sites. Their tools include ever-improving simple point-and-click applications for hacking and virus creation.

The hacker community poses a formidable challenge to your information security program. Your information security staff must be well trained and up to date on the latest security threats. By developing a better understanding of the hacker community, your staff members will be better prepared to address these issues.

Good Guys

Not everyone out there is a bad guy, though. There are also several *good guys* who can assist your organization in setting up its information security program and responding to emergencies. These organizations offer a broad range of services, including training opportunities for your staff and emergency response information to assist in the event of an attack at your company. Your information security organization should become familiar with these organizations and establish a network of third parties that they can leverage. Appendix B, "Information Security Web Sites," contains several web sites that are available for additional information. In addition, the information security industry provides a considerable amount of information through forums that your staff can leverage to stay abreast of the daily changes in the industry.

People—Administration

Everyone in the company needs to play a role for the information security program to be successful. The CEO needs to set the overall tone for the company, and each employee needs to have a basic understanding of security and must raise potential issues to management. If everyone in the company relies entirely upon the information security staff, the program will fail.

Executives need to understand the overall priorities of the program and ensure that it is meeting its objectives within their organizations. They should hold their staff accountable for meeting these objectives and evaluate the security program against other priorities for their organization when making critical resource decisions.

Security policies will impose restrictions on what organizations and employees will be able to do in certain situations. For this reason, legal and human resources departments must be actively involved in policy development. For example, your company might restrict employees from viewing inappropriate content such as pornography at work, with the penalty for violating this policy being termination of employment. Legal and human resources departments must assist in developing and communicating this policy to ensure that it does not conflict with employment laws or create an employee relations issue.

The facilities organization also needs to be involved in the development and ongoing operation of an effective security program. Access to your company's systems, offices, and restricted locations needs to be a coordinated effort. You can combine the information security and physical security functions of your company into a single organization or keep them separate, depending on your overall corporate organization. Either way, you should establish a strong relationship between these functions to ensure a successful information security program.

Table 4-3 summarizes roles that various groups in the company should assume to ensure the success of the program.

Table 4-3

Information Security Roles and Responsibilities

Key Individuals	Role in Information Security Program
■ CEO	■ Set overall tone for information security program
■ COO	■ Provide support on major initiatives
	■ Monitor overall progress of program
■ Information Security Leader:	■ Maintain information security architecture and strategy
■ Chief Information Officer (CIO)	■ Hire and manage information security team
■ Chief Security Officer (CSO)	■ Develop information security roadmap and report progress against overall objectives
■ Chief Information Security Officer (CISO)	■ Strategize and execute successful outsourcing
■ Director of Information Security	■ Ensure overall security awareness within the organization
Key Organizations	**Role in Information Security Program**
■ Board of Directors	■ Ensure that program is established within company and appropriately funded
	■ Review progress reports at quarterly meetings
	■ Require independent review of program to ensure effectiveness
■ Executive Staff	■ Sign general security policies
■ Senior Management	■ Establish priorities for information security program
	■ Measure progress against information security roadmap

continues

Key Organizations	Role in Information Security Program
■ Information Security	■ Align information technology strategy with information security strategy
■ Information Technology	■ Perform tasks outlined on information security roadmap
■ Legal	■ Work closely with information security organization to develop policies
■ Human Resources	■ Review policies to ensure that they do not conflict with labor laws
	■ Communicate policies to employees and address any employee relations issues
■ Facilities	■ Work closely with information security organization to align program with physical security strategy
	■ Coordinate day-to-day activities of providing appropriate access to both systems and work locations
■ All Employees	■ Read and follow information security policies
	■ Report security incidents

Keep in mind that each organization is quite different and that their level of involvement will vary depending upon the size and complexity of your business. A small company can combine many of these functions into one department or delegate responsibility to a single individual. Larger companies might have separate organizations that focus entirely on security-related issues. The next section presents the information security organization in more detail and provides recommendations on how to put an effective team in place.

Information Security Organization

Adhering to best practices is always a good idea when it comes to information security. Best practices prescribe a dedicated, in-house information security team, and if possible, this should be your goal. Expecting your general IT staff to cover information security in addition to other responsibilities might be unrealistic and could leave your organization exposed to threats.

Organize your security team from the executive level down, with a CIO, CSO, or CISO heading up senior-level information security managers responsible for their own security groups each designated by function. Information security organizations fall into one of two broad categories: They are usually either departments within the information technology organization or a separate information security department. For an example of an information security group within an IT department, refer to Figure 4-1.

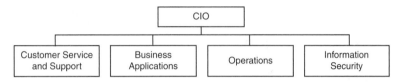

Figure 4-1 Information security as part of an IT organization.

If your information security organization falls within your company's IT department, the head of the information security organization should report directly to the department head. This ensures that information security receives the appropriate level of authority and responsibility. An alternative approach is having the information security organization report directly to the CEO or COO of the company. This raises the information security function higher in the organization and provides security managers with additional authority. Figure 4-2 provides an example of this approach.

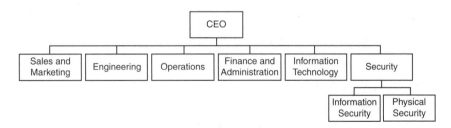

Figure 4-2 Information security as an executive-level position.

In this example, the information security organization has a peer relationship with other executives within the company and can develop a better understanding of their business priorities. Direct access to the CEO ensures that the information security program receives visibility at the executive level and that the CEO considers priorities for the program when allocating resources. The strategic importance of information security at your company will help determine the appropriate reporting relationship for your business.

Organizational Structure

From an organizational perspective, you have two principle choices regarding the structure of your team: *functional and centralized* or *geographic and decentralized*. In functional organizations, personnel remain within their areas of expertise, whether it's a part of the network topology, operating system, or a particular security product. Security personnel can focus on using and improving their technical skills.

The main advantage of the functional organization is that it enables better utilization of scarce resources. For example, it's hard to find someone who has extensive security experience in an area such as firewalls who has also deployed these devices to solve a broad range of security issues. Trying to replicate this experience across multiple geographic locations would be difficult at best. Figure 4-3 shows an example of a functional information security organization.

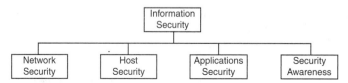

Figure 4-3 Functional information security organization.

The chief disadvantage of the functional organization structure is that the right resources are not as close to the internal customers or users because you are cutting across business units and geographies. Normally this is not a significant disadvantage because the security staff interacts directly with IT staff and doesn't deal with internal customers. Exceptions to this usually occur when the security staff is addressing a security incident or responding to business requests that conflict with security policies.

Geographic organizations have an individual who is responsible for all security requirements and components at a given location or geography. The advantage of this organizational type is that the security staff deals with the internal customers on a daily basis and can develop closer working relationships with members of customer organizations. This has a positive impact on your company's security because security personnel are in a position to "sell" the security program and encourage acceptance of policies though these relationships. See Figure 4-4 for an example of a geographic information security program.

Figure 4-4   Geographic information security organization.

The main drawback of a geographical organization is that you can quickly end up forcing your security staff to become jacks-of-all-trades. It's difficult to find someone who can develop a deep technical understanding of multiple security products that your company might deploy at a given geography. Unless you are careful, you can end up with inadequately trained security personnel spread among multiple geographies and struggling to address complex security situations.

This is one of the chief reasons that a functional organization is often preferred over a geographical one. In the performance of their duties, security personnel need to be able to resolve confrontations that occur when they disallow a request or object to a project that conflicts with existing security policies. Security personnel can resolve these situations quickly if other organizations are comfortable with their level of technical expertise and ability to address the issue.

The only way to create this level of comfort is by choosing a functional division of labor that enables security personnel to develop their technical skills and to gain experience in specific program areas. Other organizations are more likely to accept security personnel as *experts* when they concentrate on a particular function or skill set. For example, having someone who is a subject matter expert in Windows security issues makes it more likely that the IT organization will be receptive to that person's Windows security recommendations.

It's best for individual team members if you divide the functional organization into multiple areas, such as firewalls and intrusion detection, so that they can gain experience with different technologies and have some variety in their assignments.

Segregation of Duties

Segregating security groups by their designated function is one method of keeping your staff focused on its respective responsibilities. Consider separating your security staff into the following functional teams:

- **Architecture/Strategy**—This group defines the overall goals and objectives of the information security program, develops the strategies to achieve those objectives, and builds the overall implementation plan.

- **Day-to-Day Security Operations**—This team is responsible for normal day-to-day activities such as patching servers, maintaining firewall rules, and scanning the environment for vulnerabilities.

- **Compliance and Audit**—This group reviews the security program to ensure that it is working and achieving your overall objectives.

Best practices recommend that you separate the staff or team responsible for day-to-day security operations from the group responsible for compliance and audit because you don't want the "fox watching over the chicken coop."

To leverage a small but highly skilled security team, consider making the information security staff responsible for the architecture and compliance areas while assigning responsibility for the day-to-day security operations to your IT staff. Day-to-day security operations do not require as much experience as the other areas, and this strategy will enable your company to manage the size of the information security organization.

Information Security Governance Board

For your information security program to be effective, you need to establish an *Information Security Governance Board*. This group consists of cross-functional leaders who define the overall goals of the program, establish policies, and make critical decisions regarding implementation.

This board should have both the responsibility and authority to ensure that the program is successful. Often, executive leaders delegate this responsibility to the IT organization because they view information security as a "technology issue." However, increased reliance upon secure computer systems for successful business operations has raised this concern to an executive level.

The governance board should be composed of senior-level management from key organizations within your company. Information technology, human resources, legal, and facilities are essential members of this group, as are any key business units that the program affects (for example, manufacturing).

Key responsibilities for the governance board include the following:

- Establish an overall direction for the information security program.

- Ensure that the appropriate level of resources is assigned to the program.

- Assign staff members within their respective organizations to key projects.

- Establish a roadmap of planned improvements and metrics to measure the effectiveness of the program.

- Support the change required for successful implementation of the program.

- Obtain an independent review of the program by outside auditors.

- Set an example within their organizations by following information security policies.

- Provide regular reports to executive management and the board of directors on the program's status.

The leader of the board should be a senior executive; ideally, the CEO would assume this role, although this might not be possible due to time commitments. You might also consider rotating the leader of this board on a periodic basis so that each organization has an opportunity to assume this role during the course of the year.

From an administrative perspective, the initial meetings should be devoted to defining overall goals and objectives, roles and responsibilities, and processes such as metrics reporting, which will support the board. Subsequent meetings will be devoted to monitoring the progress of the program and addressing critical issues beyond the authority of lower levels within your organization. You can consider your board successful if it is able to accomplish the following:

- The security program is aligned with the overall company strategy.

- Investments are made according to overall business priorities and assessment of risks.

- A defined set of metrics for measurement of the effectiveness of the program exists.

- Industry best practices are implemented at the company and verified by independent benchmark analysis.

- An independent audit of the program is conducted on a periodic basis, and the same issues are not identified on a recurring basis.

A security governance board is an effective method of managing your information security program and obtaining the support and cooperation of key organizations within the company, and it is considered an industry best practice.

We will now review the key organizations that might comprise the governance board and their participation in the program. The first step is to obtain "buy-in" from these organizations regarding their role in the overall information security program, followed by establishing a close working relationship with each group. After establishing these relationships, you will be in a position to implement an effective governance board, and these organizations will be prepared to assume leadership roles on the board.

Information Technology

If information security is its own business unit, then obtaining buy-in from the IT department is paramount because of the huge amount of interaction between these organizations. In addition, the IT business unit will have operational control over the business' networks, the majority of the business' information systems (for example, servers), and operational or development control over the business' applications.

These areas are critical to effective information security and are exactly why your information security program requires a good working relationship with the IT business unit.

Human Resources

Company personnel are often involved in information security issues. Sometimes, an information security problem requires disciplining or terminating an employee. Thus, it's extremely important that human resources be involved in setting guidelines for employee conduct regarding security policies.

Clear policies that communicate regularly to company personnel are an important consideration in your information security program development. It's hard to get personnel to follow the information security rules when they don't know what those rules are. Legally, it's even more difficult to enforce those rules when you haven't informed personnel. Human resources must be responsible for ensuring that personnel adhere to information security policies and must assist with policy oversight and enforcement.

Legal Department

Everything that a business does must be legal, and information security is certainly no different. A legal review of information security policies and actions would be prudent in many areas of your business, so you should consider the involvement of the legal business unit as critical.

In several countries, laws concerning employee rights are much stronger than the United States. If your company operates in one of these nations, what you might like to do from an information security perspective might clash with that nation's laws. This is particularly true of such information security basics as removing an individual's access to business systems and information upon termination of employment, involuntarily or otherwise. Monitoring an employee's access to systems and information, searching a system used by an employee for evidence of inappropriate actions, and filtering web or email content are other areas that you must evaluate carefully.

Establishing a good working relationship between the information security and legal business units is essential to supporting the information security program.

Facilities

Obtaining "buy-in" from the facilities department, assuming that this department is responsible for physical security, is next on the list. Usually, information security is responsible for logical access controls to systems and services, whereas physical access controls are the responsibility of another business unit (usually facilities).

You might have a large number of local offices, and many times those local offices have logical access to your company's information system assets. Ensuring that physical security access control mechanisms are in place at those local offices is important because you don't want someone to walk right into one of your smaller offices and gain unauthorized access to your information systems.

Strong physical security access control mechanisms for your company's data centers are also critical. Your data centers are the heart of your business operations, and you should tightly control physical access so that only a small number of authorized personnel are able to enter these areas.

Physical security and information security work hand in hand to ensure that you have the necessary controls in place. Considerable involvement from this organization is essential to guarantee that you have an effective information security program.

General Business Units

Next, you need to get buy-in from various business units that are using the business applications that you are responsible for securing. Usually, these business units do not have development or operational control over these applications, but they have large end-user populations for these applications. Therefore, for your logical access controls to be effective, you must work with the various business units.

Often, getting that buy-in is a challenge. Security is typically not a priority for these business units; after all, isn't that your responsibility? In addition, no one likes to hear "no," and frequently, security personnel find themselves explaining what end users can't do. Getting the support of general business units usually requires a large education/awareness effort, often backed up by legal or regulatory requirements, firmness on your part, and patience.

People—Architecture

Continuing with the information security framework that we used to evaluate your current program, we will now define your future architecture. The industry best practices that you reviewed in this section provided some examples of a highly effective information security organization. Now you need to decide upon the appropriate information security organization for your company.

You can use Table 4-4 to summarize your desired future people architecture along with the associated priorities and desired timeframe for each area of your program. By establishing the areas on which you would like to focus your attention, you can use this information to construct an information security roadmap that is tailored to your unique business requirements.

Table 4-4

Information Security Future People Architecture					
Component	Current Score (0–2)	Desired Future Score (0–2)	Priority (High, Medium, Low)	Desired Time Frame	Comments
Strategy					
■ Written information security strategy					
■ Strategy updated on regular basis					
■ Proactive versus reactive organization					
■ Minimal impacts to business operations due to security issues					
■ Industry compliance issues (for example, HIPAA) have been addressed					
■ Industry certifications (for example, BS 7799) have been achieved					
Components					
■ Qualified leader (for example, CISSP) of organization					
■ Experienced staff with necessary training					
■ Dedicated information security staff					
■ One staff per 1,000 personnel					
■ Ongoing training program in place					
Administration					
■ Function provides regular status reports to executive staff and board of directors					

Component	Current Score (0–2)	Desired Future Score (0–2)	Priority (High, Medium, Low)	Desired Time Frame	Comments
■ Executive staff owns the information security program					
■ Active engagement with critical functions such as human resources and legal					
■ Authority to enforce information security program					
■ Performs risk analysis and management (assessments, audits, and compliance)					
Total Score (0–34)					

Grade your future program just as you graded the current program, with a "0" indicating that this practice is not important or applicable for your company, "1" indicating a partial implementation is required, and "2" for a complete implementation for this practice. Your program might require considerable improvements, and it is important to identify those areas of highest priority and the timeframe to complete these improvements. You will use this information in Chapter 7, "Information Security Roadmap," when you develop your information security roadmap.

People Summary

Having an effective information security organization is an essential component of your overall information security program. The reality is that computer systems will never be totally secure, and it is important to have a well-trained security staff in place to protect your organization as the environment changes.

Unless you have someone who is responsible for this function at your company with the necessary authority to implement your program, you will not be successful. Whether you do this with in-house staff or rely upon a third party, these personnel must have the necessary skills and an ongoing training program to ensure they are current on changes within the industry. The staff needs to work closely with leaders of key business organizations within your company and form an Information Security Governance Board to oversee the security program.

Your information security staff needs to be familiar with the changing threats to your information systems and participate with other organizations on sharing best practices to protect your company. The next chapter presents the second area of your future information security architecture: processes.

Key Points for This Chapter

- People are the most important component of your information security program and can make up for deficiencies in process and technology.

- Reporting relationships are important for information security organizations because they need the authority, in addition to responsibility, to implement programs that restrict the behavior of employees.

- The decision to develop an in-house information security program or rely upon a third party to perform these services is quite important.

- Preparing your company for industry compliance, such as Sarbanes Oxley, is quite complex, and requirements are subject to frequent change.

- Ongoing training and certification, such as CISSP, are essential if you choose to staff an in-house information security program.

- Legal and human resources departments play key roles in an effective information security program due to the restrictions that will be placed on employees and the need to follow local laws.

- Information Security Governance Boards are recommended to define the overall goals of your program, establish security processes, and make critical decisions.

Chapter 5

Process

A Fortune 500 company that is based in California failed to protect its sensitive information. A simple mistake in controls planning allowed the spread of information about executive bonuses throughout the company, angering employees about the size of executives' quarterly bonuses and embarrassing executives. It all started with printer access and naming conventions.

The human resources department in California used a printer naming convention based on characters from the TV cartoon series, The Flintstones. The printer that was used in the human resources area to print the quarterly bonus reports was called "Bam Bam" after one of the Flintstone characters. However, the company's office in Miami also decided to name one of its printers after the same Flintstones character. Because "Bam Bam" was already in use, the Miami office named their printer "Bamm Bamm." By mistake, an HR administrator printed the bonus report to "Bamm Bamm" in Miami instead of "Bam Bam" in California.

From there, information from the printed report, left lying on the printer, made its way around the company. The senior vice president of human resources got a frantic call from an executive in the Miami office (headquarters for Latin American operations) who had been handed the report. Although the HR network was sensitive, it was not treated that way. No one took enough time to think through controls and processes. No one on the HR network should have been able to print to the Miami office in the first place.

It is important to take the time to plan for security. More time and effort up front can make the difference between protecting and disclosing sensitive information. Processes are important for companies, especially when they have grown and expanded into multiple locations. This chapter reviews how to implement effective information security processes for your organization.

Introduction

Employees often consider processes a form of bureaucracy that slows everything down and prevents work from being completed. In fact, many smaller organizations are able to operate effectively with informal processes because the majority of the staff knows each other and the roles they play. As a business grows, this is no longer the case, and simple processes such as standard working hours are required for the company to be successful. The previous practice of informal processes is no longer effective because it is impossible for each employee to understand how the entire company operates.

Information security is no different. Employees need to understand their roles and expected behavior in the information security program. Developing and implementing processes takes considerable time. It's important to begin your information security processes early to lay the initial groundwork and continuously improve them over time.

Overview

Continuing with the design of your information security program, this chapter covers *information security processes*. You will continue to use the information security framework as a guide, and you will begin with a critical evaluation of your existing processes, followed by the design of your optimal future processes.

Security *processes* are the second overarching component of your security program, and *policies* are the individual elements within this component. Company policies are an important part of any effective business operation, and information security is no exception. It would be hard to imagine a business without basic policies such as normal business hours and personal time off.

Processes are like glue that binds *people* and *technology,* the other components of the information security program. This chapter introduces the essential processes that you should include in your program, many of which are best practices, and presents three key areas of your processes, including *strategy, components,* and *administration.*

Process—Strategy

Initially, you should determine whether your company has any existing information security policies and then evaluate whether your organization is complying with them. Security policies are living documents; you must review them periodically and update them to reflect changes in your enterprise and in the information security field. Often, in the absence of active enforcement, policies tend to gather dust, and due to poor communication, employees might be unaware of them. It's also likely that the policies have become outdated due to neglect.

Clarity of communication is paramount. Technical personnel might not be able to write policies that are understandable to the average employee. You might find that your policies are current but that employees are not following them simply because they do not understand them. You need to ensure that you write your policies in clear language that is easily understandable by all members of your enterprise, not just the IT and information security staff. Avoid excessive use of technical and business jargon, including obscure acronyms.

Employees must be able to reference policies whenever they have a question regarding procedures or expected behavior. Ensure that all your policies are easily accessible by employees, either through the company intranet or through any other mechanisms that you normally use to disseminate critical information (that is, break room bulletin boards). Work with your human resources organization to ensure that all new hires review and receive a copy of relevant security policies.

Your security policies should be broad in scope to ensure that they can adequately address unanticipated issues. For example, a company policy might dictate that all personal computers must have anti-virus software installed prior to employees using them for storage of customer information. However, because of its narrow scope, this policy fails to address other electronic devices, such as personal digital assistants (PDAs). The policy should have dictated that all *electronic devices* have anti-virus software installed, not just personal computers. By establishing broad policies, you avoid the need to update them frequently, and you minimize the possibility of overlooking a key area.

You should also consider risk analysis when establishing policies. It's important to have a balanced program. It's easy to err on the conservative side and establish very strict policies; however, this can undermine your security program. Employees often circumvent or ignore policies that they perceive as being inconvenient. Effective risk management strikes a balance between putting effective controls in place to protect the organization and gaining the cooperation of people who your policies affect.

Process—Components

Depending upon the size and complexity of your organization, you might have many information security policies. However, to have an effective information security program, all companies must address a few basic areas:

- **Account administration**—This is one of the most important policies, and it dictates how your organization grants access to key systems within the company. Controlling logical access to your company's information technology assets is the foundation of a successful security program.

- **Remote access**—Most personnel need to gain access to systems such as email when they are not in the office. Your remote access policy addresses this and prescribes the steps that staff must take to protect your systems when accessing them remotely.

- **Vulnerability management**—This includes evaluating your environment for known vulnerabilities or *holes* that someone can use to attack your organization. An example would be a software bug or inappropriate configuration setting that hackers can use to gain unauthorized access to your systems. Many of these vulnerabilities are well known, and automated tools are available that identify them. Your staff must address these vulnerabilities before someone finds and exploits them.

- **Acceptable use policies**—You must establish specific guidelines that define appropriate and inappropriate use of data and your information systems. This includes employees using the Internet and email systems.

- **Security awareness**—Employees need to understand their role in an effective information security program. Most employees are genuinely interested in following their company's security guidelines and only need training and reminders to aid them in following policies.

- **Emergency response**—You need to establish policies to address major unanticipated security issues. It is important to have a plan in advance, rather than simply reacting to an emergency. Defining roles and responsibilities clearly will enable your organization to recover quickly and avoid poor public relations in the event of a business disruption.

Process—Administration

Involvement of the executive staff in the development and management of information security policies is important to the effectiveness of your program. Executives need to set an example for other employees by complying with information security policies. In some cases, a security policy might restrict an employee's ability to complete his job. If your management team doesn't support (and comply) with policies, employees will ignore or find ways to circumvent them.

Human resources and your legal staff should be involved when drafting policies that affect employees. This ensures that your security policies are consistent with other company policies and do not conflict with local labor laws or employee rights. If you fail to consult these organizations, your company might violate government or industry regulations. For example, Germany has some specific restrictions on handling employee information, particularly if that information will reside outside of the country. If you conduct business there, you must consider this when drafting policies that address account management and access controls.

Unless employees understand the consequences of following key policies, you might not get their full support and cooperation. Your information security policies must clearly outline requirements for compliance and the consequences of violating these policies. Certain violations can be grounds for termination, and your policy needs to state that clearly for this to be enforced.

These are a few examples of policies that should be in operation at any company. Security processes are often informal, and the absence of clearly written policies is an indication that your program needs improvement. You can use the criteria reviewed in this section to evaluate the effectiveness of the information security processes at your company.

You can use the scorecard provided in Table 5-1 to record your evaluation of the information security processes at your company. Use the same scoring system that you have previously with your information security people evaluation: 0–2 to indicate whether the appropriate elements of your program are in place, with "0" indicating the absence of this process, "1" for partial implementation, and "2" for full implementation.

Table 5-1

Information Security Process Evaluation

Component	Score (0–2)	Comments
Strategy		
■ Written policies in consistent and easy-to-read format		
■ Easily accessible through company intranet		
■ Up-to-date with relevant changes		
■ Nontechnical and easy to understand		
■ Broad policies that cover relevant topics		
■ Incorporate risk analysis and management		
Components		
■ Account administration		
■ Remote access		
■ Vulnerability management		
■ Security awareness		
■ Emergency response		
■ Acceptable use of computers, email, and Internet		
Administration		
■ Consistent application across company		
■ Details on how policies will be monitored and enforced		
■ Active involvement of critical functions such as human resources and legal in creation of policies		
■ Multiple communication methods to disseminate policy changes		
■ Executive staff approval of policies		
Total Score (0–34)		

A score of 25 or less on this evaluation indicates that your program requires additional work to increase its overall effectiveness. In the next section, you will use the information gathered while evaluating your existing processes to design your improved information security processes.

Design of Your Future Security Processes

This section presents three major areas of information security processes: *strategy, components,* and *administration.* You will review best practices for each area, along with practical suggestions for implementing them at your company. The term *process* describes this overall component of your information security program, and *policy* describes individual elements such as security awareness.

All organizations have processes that define how they expect their employees to behave. Employees must report for work at a given hour and must work until their shift ends. Managers have guidelines that they must follow when counseling and disciplining employees that fail to follow these processes. Information security processes are similar: They define appropriate employee behavior regarding the use of key corporate assets such as computers and the information that they contain.

First you must determine which assets you are trying to protect and identify threats to these assets, and then you must assess the risks to these assets. This *information security risk analysis* will determine how you will use your information security program to protect your company's information systems.

Security Risk Analysis

It is important to conduct an inventory of assets within your company that you need to protect. This includes physical devices, including computers and servers, and intangible items, such as your company's intellectual property. You need to evaluate all these assets as a part of your *information security risk analysis* program. When conducting your analysis, focus on how essential each asset is to the day-to-day operation of your business and your company's long-term survival.

Categorize assets based upon the impact that their loss would have on your business, classifying them as mission-critical, critical, or standard. Also, consider the monetary and intrinsic value of assets when determining their importance. An asset's monetary value includes cost incurred if the asset is unavailable, the effect on your staff's productivity, and the inability of customers to reach you or use your services.

Intrinsic value is measurable by estimating the impact that an asset's loss or unavailability has on your company's credibility, reputation, and business relationships. Table 5-2 provides a high-level example of developing an inventory of your assets. As an example, the table presents physical computer assets. You might want to expand the table to cover additional physical or intangible assets.

Table 5-2

Information Security Asset Inventory

Asset	Category	Location	Comments
Client			
■ Executive staff computers	■ Critical	■ Headquarters	■ Detailed inventory developed
■ Employee computers	■ Standard	■ Worldwide	■ Only high-level inventory
■ Personal digital assistants	■ Standard	■ Worldwide	■ Unable to establish inventory
Server			
■ ERP	■ Mission-Critical	■ Headquarters	■ Detailed inventory developed
■ CRM	■ Mission-Critical	■ Headquarters	■ Detailed inventory developed
■ E-commerce	■ Mission-Critical	■ Headquarters	■ Detailed inventory developed
■ Departmental	■ Standard	■ Worldwide	■ High-level inventory only
Gateway			
■ Customer DMZ	■ Mission-Critical	■ Major geographic regions	■ Very detailed inventory
■ Partner DMZ	■ Mission-Critical	■ Major geographic regions	■ Very detailed inventory
■ Email	■ Critical	■ Major geographic regions	■ Very detailed inventory
■ Internet	■ Standard	■ Major geographic regions	■ Very detailed inventory

Some additional criteria for collecting an inventory at your company include the following:

- High-level inventory; system name, IP address, business function, operating system, physical location (site and location within data center)

- Detailed inventory; add operating system revision level, hardware model, and business owner

- Very detailed; add patch level, IT operations owner, category (for example, Mission-Critical), services running (web server versus email server)

Identify Threats to Your Assets

Threats come in many forms, and it's important both to identify a threat and determine the probability that it will create an actual *incident*. This information will enable you to identify your overall risks and develop a sound remediation plan.

Internet usage exposes companies to numerous threats from both internal and external sources. Internal threats include misuse and abuse of critical systems by employees. This includes deliberate abuse from disgruntled employees and accidental damage by well-meaning employees. Regardless of whether it's intentional, inappropriate use of Internet access results in lost productivity and ties up resources.

External threats include someone defacing your company's web site or breaking into your company's computer systems and stealing proprietary information. Viruses and worms represent an additional external threat that overlaps with an internal one: Employees failing to install or update anti-virus software can increase the likelihood that a virus will infect your systems.

Table 5-3 provides an overview of the major threat categories that exist today, along with a brief description of individual threats. Some of these threats might not apply to your company; however, it's important to understand the broad categories of potential threats so that you can determine your vulnerabilities.

Table 5-3

Major Information Security Threats

Category	Description
Impersonation/spoofing	■ Someone gains access to systems by impersonating an authorized user. ■ This can be done electronically by sending out email that appears to be a trusted party. ■ Another example would be carelessly allowing someone to learn your user ID and password.
Social engineering	■ Gaining access to confidential information through social interaction. ■ This can be anything from using fake badges to enter a building to claiming authority to an unsuspecting individual and demanding information.
Malware	Four major classes of malware: ■ Malicious virus that "infects" files on your computer. ■ Worm that is self-propagating without human interaction. ■ Trojan horse that masquerades as a useful program but actually performs malicious activity such as destroying data. ■ Spyware—software that takes control of consumers' computers or monitors their Internet use without their consent (as defined by the Federal Trade Commission).
Hacking	■ Electronically "breaking into" a company for personal gain, to cause damage, or to gain notoriety in the hacker community. ■ Common examples include defacing web sites to embarrass companies.
Denial of service	■ Direct large amounts of network traffic at systems such as web sites to overload them and prevent legitimate users from using them. ■ Distributed denial of service attacks include coordinated attacks from multiple sources that can overwhelm a system and make it unavailable to legitimate users.
Piracy and theft of intellectual property	■ Includes illegal copying and distribution of intellectual property. ■ Most common example includes unauthorized use of consumer software. ■ Stealing credit card numbers is another example of stealing personal property.

Determining Vulnerabilities

Determining how vulnerable your company is to a particular threat is the next step in the process. The objective here is to determine which areas are important to focus on. This analysis includes both monetary losses and intangible damage to reputation and brand.

It is also necessary to prioritize your vulnerabilities in terms of business impact and likelihood of exploitation. You can't protect every asset equally, and you need to base the amount of resources that you expend protecting an asset upon its value to your organization.

Although not all the threats that exist are relevant to your company now, this could easily change in the future, so it is best to reevaluate your vulnerabilities on a regular basis. You can use vulnerability management tools to automate this process and produce reports that identify potential threats. These threats might include a known "bug" in a computer program that your IT staff has not addressed. In this case, you can categorize these threats and address them based on priority.

After you've identified vulnerabilities, you should categorize them into groups based upon the urgency for mitigating them. You might divide these into groups identifying which issues you need to address within 30, 90, or 180 days and then develop recommendations for addressing or eliminating risk for each vulnerability. Based on your analysis, you can follow up with a project plan and determine staffing requirements to address these vulnerabilities.

Risk Assessment

You must assess the value of each asset against possible threats to it and the probability that you are vulnerable to a given threat. *Information security risk assessment* is similar to the analysis that actuaries in the insurance industry perform to determine premiums for automobile insurance. For example, in the case of your automobile, the value of the asset might be $40,000. Possible threats to this asset include accidents that occur while you are driving. You can determine your vulnerability to this threat by considering how many miles you drive in a given year, your previous driving record, and the geographic area where you most often drive the car.

Take inventory of your information system's assets and assess them against possible threats to understand your vulnerabilities. For example, you might have a valuable piece of intellectual property that is integral to maintaining your company's market share. The most obvious threat against this asset is theft, and the asset is very vulnerable. Perhaps all you need to do is lock the property in a safe and only give your CEO the combination. The threat remains, yet it's unlikely, that the asset will be stolen; therefore, it's less vulnerable. Although this asset was very valuable, you were able to find an inexpensive method of mitigating the risks of losing this information.

Figure 5-1 gives a graphical representation of information security risk analysis, with the left cube representing your risk before completing this analysis. The right cube represents your adjusted risk profile after applying information security risk analysis. The important thing to keep in mind is that by focusing on your most important assets and only addressing the threats that are most likely to occur, you are able to more effectively reduce your company's overall risk.

Information Security Risk Analysis

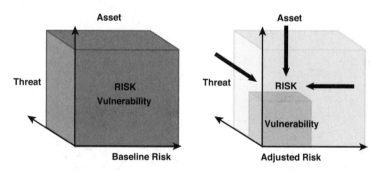

Figure 5-1   Information security risk profile.

When applying this analysis to your company's assets, focus on those areas that are critical to the long-term viability of your company. You won't completely ignore other assets, but you will place a much lower priority in those areas while you analyze your mission-critical assets. Remember, this is an iterative process, and you need to periodically reevaluate your assets and adjust the focus of your program.

Table 5-4 is an example of applying risk analysis to your asset inventory and identifying your highest areas of risk. By initially applying your resources on the high risks, you can quickly direct your program to address the highest exposures for your company.

In this example, your mission-critical servers are the areas of greatest exposure and should be the initial focus of your program. You can then proceed in a prioritized fashion to address the remaining risks in your environment. You might determine that a low risk to a standard category is acceptable and that no work is required in this area. This is a high-level view of the physical technology assets you might find in a typical company.

Table 5-4

Information Security Risk Assessment Summary

Asset	Category	Major Threats	Vulnerabilities	Risk Assessment
Client				
■ Executive staff computers	■ Critical	■ Theft	■ Security awareness	■ Medium
■ Employee computers	■ Standard	■ Viruses	■ Virus definition update process	■ Low
■ Personal digital assistants	■ Standard	■ Theft	■ Security awareness	■ Low
Servers				
■ ERP, CRM	■ Mission-Critical	■ Impersonation	■ Account administration process	■ High
■ E-commerce	■ Mission-Critical	■ Hacking	■ Patch management	■ Medium
■ Email	■ Critical	■ Viruses	■ Virus definition update process	■ Low
■ Departmental	■ Standard	■ Social engineering	■ Security awareness	■ Low

continues

Asset	Category	Major Threats	Vulnerabilities	Risk Assessment
Gateway ■ Customer–partner DMZ ■ Email ■ Internet	■ Mission-Critical ■ Critical ■ Standard	■ Denial of service ■ Viruses ■ Impersonation	■ Overall security architecture ■ Virus definition update process ■ Account administration process	■ High ■ Low ■ Low

Process—Strategy

Information security policies, standards, and procedures are different documents that all need to work together to support the process component of an information security program. Figure 5-2 shows an overview of these documents.

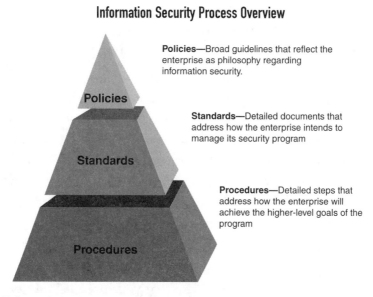

Figure 5-2   Information security program process overview.

Each enterprise has unique factors that it needs to consider when developing its own processes; these include company size, complexity, and industry.

Things to Consider

Creating an effective security policy is a balancing act—employees must have access to the information assets they need to do their jobs and stay productive. At the same time, you must maintain the integrity and confidentiality of your company's data. Each policy must be sensitive to varying global cultures and regulations and be consistent across all offices. After you have determined the scope and goals of your policy effort, here are some things that you should consider when you are developing a policy:

- **Policy format**—The needs of your enterprise will determine the format of your policy. Many enterprises have 20 or more policies in place at one time. As an example, a policy might declare that your enterprise will comply with all government and industry regulations 30 days in advance of the deadline. In this case, you would set standards and procedures for how you would go about meeting the terms of each government and industry regulation to which your enterprise is subject (such as HIPAA or GBLA).

- **Dynamic nature**—You might have a policy in place, but when is the last time you updated it? Policies are not static documents. As operating environments, business plans, regulations, and the economics of your enterprise change, you should update your policy to reflect these changes. If you create your program with a general policy for each area, supported by specific standards and procedures, changes to policy will be easier because you will only need to change the individual standards or procedures, not the overall policies for the program.

- **Avoid long technical documents**—Security policies should be concise and written in a way that all employees can understand, even those that lack technical knowledge. To ensure that your policies are clear and understandable, you might consider having your corporate communications organization assist with the final review of all policies.

- **Provide details regarding monitoring and enforcement**—Clearly state how your organization will monitor policy and the penalties for employees who fail to comply.

Communicating the Policy

Enterprise-wide communication is necessary for a policy to be effective. It is your responsibility to make sure that everyone understands their role in security initiatives. Here are some things that you can do to improve communication and employee compliance:

- **Educate employees**—Inform your employees about various security issues, from information misuse to proper use of email to physical security. Your employees will better understand the security policy and their important role in the overall security of the enterprise. Covering this topic in new hire orientation and providing refresher training every year is an effective way of keeping staff informed.

- **Make it accessible**—All employees need to know where to find security policies. Make the policy easily accessible through email, an employee handbook, or your intranet so that employees can access it at a moment's notice. Whenever you make updates to the policy, give employees an explanation of the changes.

- **Get signatures**—Have your employees sign and date the policy, with their signature being a testament to their understanding and willingness to comply with its terms. Most people want to understand things before they sign them, so chances are that your employees will take time to study the policy more carefully if they are required to sign it. When requesting their signatures, let your employees know that this is not an indication of lack of trust, but rather that you need them to understand the importance of the program. Carefully evaluate the cultural impacts of requesting signatures prior to making this part of your program.

- **Have incident response procedures in place**—Employees should know to whom they should report and what actions they should take if security breaches occur. Make the process simple to encourage employees to report incidents.

Process—Components

Essential processes that apply to companies of all sizes include account administration, security awareness, emergency response, vulnerability scanning, and acceptable use. This section provides an in-depth review of these processes and offers some suggestions for implementing them at your company.

Account Administration

It is important to have controls in place governing who has access to your information systems. These controls must address everyone who wants access to the systems, from full-time to temporary employees, and must grant access rights based upon job function, granting access only to areas that employees and contractors must access to perform their jobs.

Ensure that employees and contractors who leave the company have their access revoked quickly; you don't want to leave your organization vulnerable to a disgruntled employee. Finally, passwords should follow industry best practices for length (that is, minimum of 8 characters) and use of special characters (for example, #), and staff should update them on a regular basis (that is, every 90 days). Having processes in place to track people is essential for all these controls to be effective.

Probably the single most important security process for businesses today is keeping track of employees and contractors, their employment status, access rights, and so on. How do you know who is at your company legitimately? What capacity are they in—are they an employee, a contractor, a vendor, a temp, or a consultant? Without this information, how do you assign them the proper roles from a security perspective? If you can't do that, you will not have an effective security program.

The following is a real-world example of this issue. At a board of directors meetings at a multibillion-dollar company in Silicon Valley, the head of the HR department and the CFO often disagreed about the total number of personnel in the company. The impression was that the head of HR didn't care about the number of nonemployees, so she did not account for them. The board became furious with both the head of HR and the CFO because they never had an accurate count of employees versus nonemployees, nearly all of whom were receiving physical and logical access to the company's assets and pay.

It doesn't matter how good your security staff or processes are. If you don't know how many and what types of employees you have, you have a real problem. You will never be able to determine who should have access and which types and levels are appropriate.

One best practice for account administration is entering all staff, regardless of status, into a *human resources information system* (HRIS). Human resources can then run a report of how many employees and nonemployees are at the company. If people are not in the HRIS, they

- Do not get paid, which usually gets someone's attention

- Do not receive a badge that grants them physical access to facilities

- Do not receive access to business information systems at the company

HR has to make sure it includes every employee and nonemployee in the HRIS, including other information such as non-English names, common names, and preferred names. For example, many Asian employees adopt an English name as their preferred name, yet their employee documentation (payroll, HRIS, and so on) has their birth names. If HR doesn't document all this information, confusion can result when their email addresses, user names, and facilities badges have their preferred names instead of birth names.

To remedy this situation, HR must assign unique personnel numbers to all staff members, regardless of their employment status. By assigning a personnel number, companies can definitively track personnel. The addition of a letter code for quick determination of employment status, such as *E* for *employee* or *C* for *contractor*, will also assist in the process. This personnel number remains with the individual, even if that person resigns or is terminated. If the person is rehired, the old/original number is reinstated/reactivated.

HR generally knows when it is hiring or firing someone. However, this is not always the case with nonemployees because your company might not require HR to keep track of those personnel. Because HR might have little or no knowledge of when nonemployees leave, you should define processes for tracking nonemployees to ensure that you revoke their access when they leave.

Consider isolating all nonemployee accounts from employee accounts including their badge access because you will probably want to administer these staff separately. For example, a good practice is to set these accounts to expire after 90 days unless an employee's manager tells HR to revalidate the individual and tells IT to extend that person's access.

These are just a few examples of the importance of account administration processes and how you might implement them at your company to ensure that your company's assets are secure.

Security Awareness

Security awareness is a key component of your information security processes. Employees need to understand their role in the overall security program; this includes a general education on information security and what actions you expect from employees. Security policies can restrict employee's behavior, so it is important to explain the reasons for each security measure.

You might have a policy that dictates that passwords must be a certain length and contain special characters. An employee might not want to do this; after all, it's easier to use a common word or a pet's name. If you explain to employees that *password cracking* programs exist that use dictionaries of commonly used words to crack passwords, they will understand why they must follow this policy. To promote acceptance of the policy, you can also provide simple, easily understood guidelines on how to establish effective passwords.

Remember that employees need to understand what you expect from them and why. Most employees are genuinely interested in doing what is right and will comply with polices when they understand them better. On the other hand, it's almost impossible to get personnel to follow rules if they don't know what those rules are or why they exist. Therefore, security awareness is extremely important for getting cooperation and compliance.

Security awareness should be done professionally and creatively. Show ingenuity in the way you present and communicate the message, using email reminders, posters in prominent areas (such as lobbies, corridors, cafeterias, lunchrooms, elevators, and entranceways), web portals, and electronic articles.

Avoid the tired old message of, "Do this; don't do that." The message must be relevant and creative to get people's attention and acceptance. Tailor your messages to the environment; you can separate environments by geography or by business functions. For instance, a security awareness program for software development personnel will have little impact if all the examples presented focus on a manufacturing environment.

These security awareness messages help ensure that in the event of an emergency, your staff will know how to respond. As we have mentioned, best practices in this area include security awareness training during new employee orientation and ongoing refresher training on an annual basis.

By explaining these issues to new employees, you can educate them on expected behavior and the importance of security at the company. Refresher training is important because information security changes on a regular basis, and it is quite possible that employees aren't familiar with recent threats and their role in protecting the company. Senior management must set the tone for the security program by complying with security policies.

Emergency Response

If your systems are hit by a virus and are knocked offline for 24 hours or more, what would you do? Best practices include a predefined checklist of procedures that staff must carry out during a security emergency. Among other things, the checklist should provide clear guidelines for communication, including whom staff members need to inform and how employees can reach them at all times. It is a good idea to engage your legal, public relations, and human resources departments in this preparation. Chances are that something will happen, and you will be glad that you have prepared for it.

Emergency response is about responding professionally and coherently. To respond effectively, you need to do some work before an emergency occurs. Key elements include the following:

- **Planning**—In an emergency, it's easy to overlook key issues and responsibilities, and you might fail to coordinate properly, resulting in duplicated or even counterproductive efforts. Having a contingency plan in place enables you to mitigate damage. Best practices call for quarterly drills to ensure that your plan is up to date and that it will work when you need it.

- **Simplicity**—Your plan needs to be thorough yet straightforward. Limit your plan to a couple of pages that summarize your actions in the event of an emergency.

- **Articulate**—Your plan needs to articulate what your staff needs to do in a clear and concise manner. Detail which role is responsible for each action, but don't try to write an emergency response procedure that's going to cover every single contingency. Even if you had the time for this kind of plan, you'd find that technology, processes, and people change often at your company, so you must continually adjust the plan. Focus on the high-level activities that your staff should address, such as restoring the mission-critical applications as soon as possible.

- **Role-based versus Individual-based**—Define the responsibilities in general business areas and base them on roles, not individuals. Don't list individual people in the plan—if Bob's role is *network administrator,* the plan should state that the network administrator is responsible. That way, no one will need to call Bob if he's in Hawaii.

- **Communication**—How will you communicate? Don't assume that your office or mobile phone will be working in an emergency. Many people assume that notification alerts will come through email, yet if a virus takes down your network, that avenue of communication will be closed. Make sure that your emergency response plan includes multiple and redundant communication methods, such as phones, pagers, faxes, *and* email.

- **Authority**—Senior management needs to establish who has authority to do what in an emergency. Who actually has the authority to declare an emergency or decide that it has passed? An emergency is not the time to argue over seniority and scope of authority. You must establish this in advance.

Your emergency response plan should provide simple, easy-to-follow procedures that your staff can use during any security crisis that your company might encounter in the future. It is important to test these procedures periodically to ensure that your team is ready in the event of an emergency.

Your emergency response process is one component of an overall business resumption plan that is outside the scope of this book. The process outlined previously only relates to what is required from a security perspective and does not address many of the broader issues that you must address to ensure business continuity in the event of a disaster.

Vulnerability Management

Vulnerability management is an important component of your information security processes. By developing a regular program of physically reviewing components of your overall environment, commonly referred to as scanning, you can identify vulnerabilities and establish priorities for remediation.

Scanning is important because it indicates how well various teams are securing your assets by hardening servers and clients and avoiding security issues. Through scanning, you and your staff can address known vulnerabilities and stay on top of things like applying patches.

It is important to develop a regular schedule for running network scans and to designate which members of the staff will be responsible for running these scans. Key considerations for these processes include the following:

- **Frequency**—Vulnerability management scanning should be performed regularly, at a minimum of once per quarter. Performing scans more often than quarterly for noncritical systems is an operational hindrance. Scanning less frequently than quarterly is unacceptable because network and system configurations are too dynamic, and the risk to your environment due to the lack of knowledge about vulnerability status is too great. If you have the capability to perform vulnerability management scanning in-house, do so, but third-party validation is a good check of your program's effectiveness.

- **Schedule**—Having a schedule ensures that scanning is performed on a regular basis. Inform essential personnel in network and operations roles of the schedule. Limiting knowledge of the schedule to essential personnel ensures that your staff will not assume that *actual* malicious traffic is associated with vulnerability management scanning and ignore it.

- **Results**—Make the scan results available to the staff who is responsible for keeping those systems up-to-date. To further ownership of the remediation process, break reports down by ownership of systems. A single report containing a large number of systems belonging to multiple individuals is difficult to work with. It is much better to have clear ownership over these systems so that you can hold individuals accountable.

- **Progress**—You need some way to track progress or the lack thereof. Progress must be made session over session or scan over scan so that you can be sure that actual remediation is taking place. Repeatedly finding the same vulnerabilities on the same systems is not good. Reports need to identify the status of remediation so that you can tell whether personnel have made progress.

Personnel usually perform scanning from a network-based perspective; however, staff can also scan from a host-based perspective by placing an agent on each host. A network-based scan looks at your systems from the outside, as a hacker might, whereas a host-based scan looks at the system from the inside. Host-based scanning is more cumbersome, but it can give you a better view of system vulnerabilities. Network-based scanning is easier to conduct, but it does not give you as much information as host-based scanning.

You should subject mission-critical and external-facing systems to network- and host-based scans while limiting all other systems to just network-based scans. Scanning is a snapshot in time, as opposed to an ongoing or continual assessment of your system's vulnerability; nonetheless, it provides a view of how systems look from a known vulnerability perspective. In addition, you should mandate vulnerability management for the introduction of new applications to ensure that they do not introduce unexpected vulnerabilities.

Acceptable Use

An acceptable use policy covers all corporate assets used by employees, including Internet, email, computers, and phones. This is an important policy because employees often consider their computer personal as opposed to company property. You should have heavy involvement of the human resources and legal organizations because this policy will restrict employees' behavior, and you need to communicate this to them clearly. Key considerations include the following:

- **Data protection**—Make clear that it is the employee's responsibility to protect the information stored on his computer. This includes critical information such as customer names and addresses because it would be embarrassing (and possibly illegal) to have this information fall into the wrong hands.

- **Nonbusiness use**—Employees must understand the limits of nonbusiness use of company email and Internet resources. This includes visits to inappropriate web sites such pornography, hate, and gambling sites and the use of company email for personal or inappropriate use because your company's name will be part of the email address.

- **Policy violations**—Specify which activities will be considered offensive and in violation of the policy and the consequences for violating these policies.

- **Safeguarding their computers**—Require password protection, lock computers when they're not in use, and create reasonable measures to prevent theft.

- **Unauthorized software**—Restrict use of nonbusiness software, downloading unauthorized software, or file sharing. This can interfere with business applications and information security products, and it increases the support costs of computers when these products cause problems. The use of unlicensed software is a particular concern because it can expose the company to litigation.

Remote Access

Enterprise networks span multiple geographies, and employees access them remotely on a regular basis. Having a strong remote access policy in place is essential. First, you should determine who can access systems remotely and then how they connect to the company network. Clearly define security measures that remote users must follow, including anti-virus and firewall protection.

- **Authorization**—Spell out whom you will allow to access systems remotely and what approval is required. Best practices grant remote users access based upon roles and restrict access by nonemployees.

- **Information**—What limitations have you placed on information that employees can access remotely? Is access restricted to common applications such as email, or can employees use sensitive systems such as payroll, too? You should encrypt information that employees access remotely to prevent unauthorized access during transmission, and encrypt critical data on the remote device in case the device becomes lost or stolen.

- **Access Methods**—The broad availability of high-speed access outside of the office requires your policies to spell out the acceptable methods for accessing systems remotely. Clear standards are required to ensure adequate security and a reasonable level of support to these users.

- **Home Computers**—Allowing employees to access a corporate network using a home computer raises several issues. These include the problems of storing and protecting critical company information downloaded onto an employee's home computer and what to do if the employee leaves the company. Best practice in this area is to disallow the use of a home computer for remote connection because numerous issues can result from this practice, although a company-issued laptop can be an exception.

These are some of the considerations for putting an effective remote access policy in place. Remember that it is much easier to put controls in place when employees physically work in the office because you can easily identify who they are and ensure that they have adequate protection on their computers.

This all changes when someone works remotely. You don't want someone impersonating an employee and gaining unauthorized access to your systems. We will review some of the technology components that are required in this area later in the next chapter.

Components Summary

These information security processes represent a subset of what is required at your company. However, they are important, and you should consider developing them first. After you have some of the basics in place, it is easier to build on this foundation and develop additional policies.

Process—Administration

The fact that information security processes will restrict employee behavior will cause concerns within organizations. Employees don't like anyone telling them what they can and cannot do. Usually they are primarily concerned with getting their job done, and they resent additional steps for the sake of security. As we have mentioned, administration is a careful balancing act between placing too many constraints on employees (which can motivate them to circumvent controls) and not securing systems adequately.

Using an appropriate use policy as an example, it's not a problem to prevent employees from accessing pornography, gambling, and hate sites because these could easily be considered an inappropriate use of the company's systems. On the other hand, if you expand this list to online shopping, an employee might be prevented from purchasing office-related supplies on the Internet. The objective is to find the optimal balance that protects the company but that doesn't result in an uproar among employees.

Follow a consistent process when establishing information security policies. A cross-functional team with representatives from information security, human resources, legal, and business units such as sales and marketing should be responsible for drafting and maintaining processes. Ideally, these organizations would be part of a formal *security governance process* (see Chapter 4, "People") that oversees the program and approves policies.

Circulate draft policies among a broad cross section of employees for comments and suggestions before implementation. Finally, set aside time for communications of new policies because employees must understand them. You should also provide ongoing refresher training to ensure that employees are aware of new and existing policies.

Measuring Compliance

It is difficult to know whether employees are following your information security policies unless you set up a program to measure compliance. One solution is to use an internal or external audit team to measure policy compliance. If it is an internal team, make sure they are not the same organization in charge of defining and enforcing policy. Segregation of roles is important in this area. Products and tools are available that will automatically monitor and manage the discovery of policy compliance or deviations and vulnerabilities on the enterprise network.

Set an Example

Involve your human resources and legal departments when setting policies because it helps them understand and promote the policies on your behalf. Getting buy-in from other departments and executives is essential because it increases company-wide support and awareness for your security initiatives. Establishing a formal *information security governance board* ensures that representatives from key business units are involved in the program and are responsible for reviewing and approving policies.

Ultimately, your employees look to you for a positive example. Senior management must set a good example by conspicuously complying with these policies. You can change attitudes and bring more attention to security by making it a major enterprise concern. Provide security education for your employees to help them become more security-aware. Through education, you can reiterate the importance of every person's contribution in making the security practice a success.

Make security an everyday theme and a part of the daily routine at your enterprise. To encourage everyone's participation, acknowledge or reward exemplary policy-compliant behavior, such as prompt reporting of an incident.

Consistency

When creating any policy, make sure it is consistent on a global basis. For instance, some data protection laws in Europe are more stringent than laws in the United States. This requires that you create a policy that complies with European rules and implement it across all your offices worldwide. If you conduct business over the Internet, other companies from all over the world have access to your business, so you need to be aware of and comply with international regulations when conducting business across borders, even virtual ones.

Future Process Architecture

Now you can define your future processes using the information security framework. The best practices described in this chapter provided you with examples of a highly effective program. You can use the scorecard in Table 5-5 to summarize your desired future process architecture. Use the same scoring methodology that we previously described, with "0" for not implementing this practice, "1" for partial implementation, and "2" for full implementation.

Table 5-5

Information Security Future Process Architecture					
Component	Current Score (0–2)	Desired Future Score (0–2)	Priority (High, Medium, Low)	Desired Time Frame	Comments
Strategy					
▪ Written policies in consistent and easy-to-read format					
▪ Easily accessible through company intranet					
▪ Up-to-date with relevant changes					
▪ Nontechnical and easy to understand					
▪ Broad policies that cover relevant topics					
▪ Incorporate risk analysis and management					
Components					
▪ Account administration					
▪ Remote access					
▪ Vulnerability management					
▪ Security awareness					
▪ Emergency response					
▪ Acceptable use of computers, email, and Internet					
Administration					
▪ Consistent application across company					
▪ Details on how policies will be monitored and enforced					
▪ Active involvement of critical functions such as HR and legal in creation of policies					
▪ Multiple communication methods to disseminate policy changes					

continues

Component	Current Score (0–2)	Desired Future Score (0–2)	Priority (High, Medium, Low)	Desired Time Frame	Comments
■ Executive staff approval of policies					
Total Score (0–34)					

When completing this scorecard, it is also important to prioritize improvement areas because you will not be able to work on all elements of the program at the same time. Also include the desired timeframe for achieving the future score because you will use the combination of this information for developing your future information security architecture.

Process Summary

We examined guidelines for establishing and enforcing information security processes at your company, along with relevant industry best practices. It's important to reiterate that employees generally do not like to be constrained; establishing processes is a balancing act between maximizing staff productivity and ensuring that an embarrassing security incident doesn't occur.

You must put metrics in place to monitor the progress of your program because you will make considerable investments in this area and it is important to demonstrate results. Next, you will move on to the third element of your program that you will use to enforce policies within your program: *technology.*

Key Points for This Chapter

■ Information security processes are similar to other company rules, such as normal working hours or personal time off, and you should outline acceptable behavior for members of your organization.

- Security processes must be clear and accessible so that everyone understands his responsibilities in areas such as acceptable use of computers for business purposes and implications of inappropriate behavior, such as downloading pornography.

- Security risk analysis should be performed to inventory your organization's assets and to determine those that should be provided the highest level of protection, such as your critical business systems.

- Security processes should anticipate changes and should be broad in scope, such as covering personal digital assistants in addition to personal computers.

- Account administration is the most basic security process and can be compared to providing office keys in the physical security world.

- Active involvement of critical functions such as human resources and legal are essential for administration of security processes.

Chapter 6

Technology

A multibillion-dollar international oil company discovered that one of its internal file servers had been compromised. Had an internal employee compromised the system, or had the network been compromised by an external party? The company didn't know, and it opened an investigation to find out. The credentials used to gain access to the system were fraudulent, so the investigation focused on the authentication servers and discovered that two of them had been compromised.

The company's internal network was complex, and critical nodes were not adequately secured, so the authentication systems served little purpose. The soft, chewy center of the large, complex network was unprotected.

It took months to trace the sequence of events. Initially, a web server on the company's extranet was compromised. Then the intruder exploited a misconfigured firewall on the extranet to gain access to the company's intranet. When on the intranet, the intruder compromised a fileserver and then found the authentication servers, compromising two of them. The unauthorized party was then able to masquerade on the intranet and access unauthorized systems and data.

With valuable and extremely sensitive information on that intranet, such as where the focus of future oil exploration should be, stronger internal security measures should have been in place. This company made large investments in its information security program and was still successfully compromised by an unauthorized party. This chapter describes how to leverage your information security technology investments to protect your organization.

Introduction

Successful deployment of technology requires a thoughtful architecture that deploys tools in a calculated manner. Unfortunately, it's possible to invest large amounts of money in this area and yet produce little or no results.

Your company might have invested in the most secure firewall product available; however, if your staff doesn't configure the device correctly, it won't protect your assets. In fact, it might contribute to the threat. Poorly implemented technological solutions are often the source of many security issues. It is much more important to deploy a few products successfully than to attempt to implement all possible security products at your company.

Overview

Technology is the third and final component of your information security program. Of course, technology is only effective when your staff implements it correctly and has processes and procedures in place to ensure that it remains effective.

Using the information security framework, you will first evaluate your current technology environment, followed by a design of your future desired environment. You will assess technology strategy, components, and administration to determine the effectiveness of your program.

Technology—Strategy

Evaluating your existing information security architecture provides some indication of how well your staff has planned and implemented the technology component of your program. The dynamic nature of business and information security challenges requires that your organization update the information security architecture on a regular basis.

Does the existing technology architecture allow for planned growth? Expanding your business model to rely more upon Internet sales and distribution requires a much different strategy from traditional order fulfillment through retail stores.

Your architecture should also address the best practices of separating your environment into *zones* and *layering* your security. *Digital zones* enable your customers and partners to access portions of your environment to conduct business while still restricting access to your critical systems. Layering your security, or *defense-in-depth,* is a principle that you should use to protect your gateways, servers, and clients.

Review how much activity your staff devotes to tactical activities as opposed to strategic improvements; this can provide some indication of how well the staff planned the architecture and your organization's ability to implement it. If your staff is constantly engaged in *firefighting mode,* your program strategy needs some improvements.

Review these basic information security concepts for an indication of the effectiveness of your program.

Technology—Components

The technologies deployed at your company will vary based upon the complexity of your business and the maturity of your information security program. The most basic technologies that every company should use include *authentication, authorization, and accounting* (AAA).

In addition, every company needs anti-virus software and firewalls; both are an important part of a layering strategy. New viruses appear daily, and unless you have this protection in place, your information systems are at risk. Provide anti-virus protection at three levels (layers): gateway, server, and individual computers, also called *clients*. Firewalls are necessary to ensure that only authorized messages or *traffic* enter and leave your computing infrastructure.

Vulnerability management and intrusion detection tools work together as proactive and reactive protection. Proactively, you can use vulnerability management tools to evaluate (*scan*) your environment and identify vulnerabilities that you must address. Like viruses, new vulnerabilities appear on an almost daily basis, and these tools identify these vulnerabilities so that your staff can address them. Intrusion detection tools are *reactive* in that they indicate when inappropriate activity has taken place within your computing environment.

Several other information technology tools exist, including remote access controls, content filtering, and security management; these are reviewed in more detail later in this chapter. You might find it necessary to have these additional tools deployed to protect your business.

In a small company with a single person devoted to security, it might not be practical to deploy these tools in addition to the basic tools mentioned previously. In addition, if you have chosen to hire a third party to manage all or part of this technology, you should evaluate that organization's ability to support your requirements in this area.

Technology—Administration

Just having these tools deployed isn't an automatic indication that your staff has implemented them correctly or is maintaining them adequately. Independent evaluation of your program is an important part of reviewing your current environment. This includes an overall review of your program each year and periodic *penetration* testing to ensure that an unauthorized party cannot gain access to your systems. Penetration testing refers to trying to penetrate security from the outside in the same fashion as a hacker.

It is also critical to review the progress your organization has made toward implementing the recommendations provided during these evaluations. If the same issues continue to appear on consecutive reports, this is an indication that your staff isn't making sufficient progress.

It's difficult to determine if you are making progress unless you have a process in place to measure how effective your program is. Metrics reporting is critical, and you should provide these reports to the executive management team and the board of directors. Their active involvement ensures that the appropriate priority and funding are devoted to the program.

Change management is another critical process that you should use to introduce updates into your computing environment without creating unexpected problems. A static environment is easy to protect; however, most environments change on a daily basis. These changes can include everything from adding system accounts for employees to updating firewall configurations. Unless you have change management procedures in place, it will be difficult to determine the impact that these changes have on your program.

Use Table 6-1 to evaluate the technology component of your information security program, using the 0–2 scoring method, with "0" representing the absence of this practice, "1" for partial implementation, and "2" for full implementation.

Table 6-1

Information Security Technology Evaluation		
Component	Score (0–2)	Comments
Strategy		
■ Comprehensive information security architecture		
■ Computing environment segmented into security zones		
■ Security layered at gateway, server, and client		
■ Security roadmap includes both strategic and tactical objectives		
■ Strategy supports current models for conducting business		
Components		
■ AAA		
■ Anti-virus		
■ Firewalls		
■ Vulnerability management		
■ Intrusion detection		
Administration		
■ Regular scanning and remediation program		
■ Quarterly penetration testing		
■ Annual independent audit of security program		
■ Regular update of anti-virus definitions		
■ Change management		
■ Reporting on security incidents and initiatives to executive management and board of directors		
Total Score (0–32)		

A score of 25 or less indicates that the technology component of your program requires improvement. By leveraging the security evaluation framework, you can easily focus your improvements in these areas. You should take into account the size of your company because your staff might not have the time or experience to effectively deploy all these tools; we will offer some suggestions later in this chapter on possible alternatives.

Design of Your Future Security Technology

Technology is the final element of your program and often the most confusing. Many companies place too much emphasis on technology, which can lead to a false sense of security, especially when it's so easy to deploy these tools incorrectly.

Technology—Strategy

After you have determined which critical assets you want to protect, you can determine the appropriate technology to deploy. Technology is a key component of your information security program. You can use it to enforce your security processes and guide employee behavior. Technology is important, but no matter how good it might be, it won't overcome weak processes or weak security personnel. If you don't have the people and processes in place, you don't need the technology.

This section begins with a review of your overall technology architecture and builds upon the concepts that were introduced in the previous chapter. Individual technology components are reviewed, along with practical suggestions for deploying these devices at your company. Technology gaps are examined, followed by additional security challenges that you will face when managing your program.

Overall Architecture

Previously, the word *perimeter* was used to describe the digital boundaries between the internal corporate network and the outside world, typically the Internet. However, the terminology has evolved to reflect the significantly more complex digital relationships that enterprises have with their customers, partners, and suppliers. Enterprises talk about securing specific *gateways* or places where their networks connect with outside systems.

The fundamental goal of protecting an enterprise from threats originating outside organizational boundaries hasn't changed. However, whereas in the past a typical enterprise would have just one connection (gateway) leading to the Internet or other external systems, today's networks have dozens of connections. The so-called perimeter is now too porous to protect with a single firewall. You must use multiple security products and techniques to ensure that every gateway is secure.

Today's challenge is finding a way to meet the growing demand for remote access to networks while maintaining their security. Remote users not only include employees, many of whom work remotely, but also customers, business partners, and suppliers, who are given limited network access. Added to this are contractors, consultants, temporary workers, or vendor personnel who work at your company on any given day. Many of these personnel also need some level of network privilege, perhaps for only a brief period.

Two major architectural concepts introduced in the first chapter include separating your company's computing infrastructure into *digital zones* and defense-in-depth by *layering* your security at the gateway, server, and client. Figure 6-1 provides a high-level view of the major digital zones that comprise a typical enterprise.

Information Security Overall Architecture

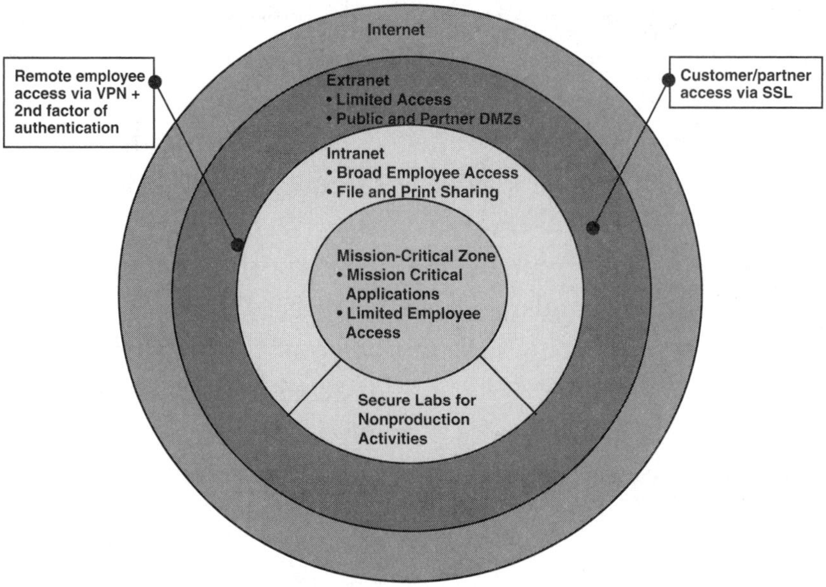

Figure 6-1   Information security program overall architecture.

Digital Zones

The objective is to divide your environment into separate zones, each with differing levels of security and authorization required to access that portion of your computing infrastructure. These zones include the Internet, your *extranet* (where your customers and partners are able to access), the *intranet* for employees, and the *mission-critical zone*, which is the most secure portion of your environment. A firewall separates the zones and restricts access to include authorized staff only.

In Figure 6-1, the outermost circle represents the Internet. It's important to put a layer of protection such as a firewall between your business and this area. The next circle is the *extranet,* where the only people who have access are customers and trusted vendors with whom you conduct business. They have limited access to this area in the form of electronic keys (user IDs and passwords) that permit them to enter this zone.

The extranet separates your company from the Internet. One of the common questions asked in security is, "Should I care about anything outside of my exterior firewalls?" The answer is yes. By having an intrusion detection system external to your network, you can collect valuable intelligence about what type of attacks hackers launch at your company.

Of course, this is a second priority to making sure that your network is secure and that no attacks are successful. It's a balancing act, and organizations that have more mature security programs are in a better position to pursue this strategy.

Extranet

Organizations often separate their extranet into distinct zones to allow their customers and partners access to their computing environment. Depending upon your company, you might choose to deploy multiple distinct extranet zones. The purpose of an extranet is to allow customers access to one section of your network while keeping them segregated from the majority of your enterprise systems. In the event that a hacker compromises the extranet, he is kept from accessing the rest of your infrastructure.

Access controls, including user IDs and passwords, are needed to access these systems. Secure Sockets Layer (SSL) technology encrypts any information that is transferred while customers use these systems. Your company might have multiple extranets for various customers and partners in addition to geographic extranets due to the high cost of network bandwidth in some parts of the world.

Because extranets connect to the Internet, it is a good idea to deploy the following security devices to protect these environments:

- Network-based intrusion detection
- Network-based vulnerability management
- Host-based intrusion detection
- Host-based vulnerability management

You can use proactive vulnerability management tools to identify known security issues that generally have well-understood solutions, such as vendor patches or configuration changes. Intrusion detection tools are reactive and alert your information security staff that something unusual is happening in your environment, which might indicate an attack. These tools complement each other in protecting your environment.

Intranet

Your intranet is where your employees conduct the majority of their day-to-day work. Access to this area is restricted to employees, contractors, and temporary staff. You should separate this area from your extranet with a firewall and limit traffic that passes between them.

The innermost area of your enterprise contains mission-critical systems such as your enterprise resource planning (ERP) system and customer relationship management (CRM) systems that only a limited number of your staff is able to access.

If you allow remote access to your interior perimeter at all, you should require *two-factor* authentication. The first factor of authentication is normally user IDs and passwords, and the second is often a unique identifier such as a *security token* (often a *smart card*) that confirms your identity.

Finally, you might have areas of your intranet segregated into labs for your engineering staff so that they can perform their design and testing without disrupting other portions of the business.

Mission-Critical Zone

This is the core of your computing environment, so you should provide the highest level of protection to this area. This is where all your applications and systems that are essential to running your business reside.

You should deploy the full suite of intrusion detection and vulnerability management tools to protect this core part of your business operations. Restrict access to this area and put controls in place to ensure that your staff receives the appropriate approvals prior to granting someone access to these systems.

Secure Labs for Nonproduction Activities

Many engineering organizations need to work without the restrictions that you would find in a business production environment. Software companies need to test their products and simulate conditions that might cause the products to fail. Engineers can't conduct these tests in any of the zones that we described earlier because doing so could have an adverse impact on business operations.

To support these needs, you can create individual engineering labs and use firewalls to segregate them from the rest of the business. This can help prevent any work performed within the labs from crossing into other portions of your network environment. This strategy enables the engineering staff to complete its work and removes any risks that these activities might prevent the company from conducting its day-to-day business operations.

It is a best practice for the information technology organization to manage these firewalls because they are responsible for protecting your company's assets. Allowing the engineering staff to manage access to the company's production environment could lead to problems. Your personnel use the production network to run your business, and it's extremely important that this network is protected and stable. Testing and stability do not go hand in hand.

Defense-in-Depth

An alternative view of the *digital zones* of the business is to separate your environment into three layers: *gateways, servers,* and *clients.* Depending upon the size of your company, you might have hundreds or even thousands of these devices. Figure 6-2 provides a graphical view of the three layers of security that are required for your enterprise; these layers might or might not coincide with a particular zone.

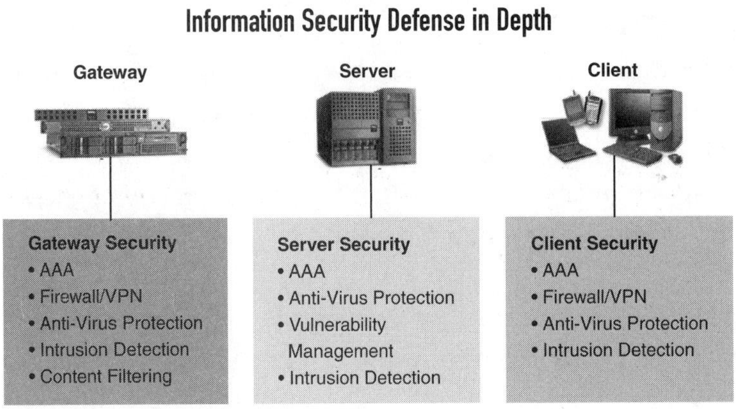

Information Security Defense in Depth

Figure 6-2   Security defense-in-depth.

Gateway

The simplest explanation of a gateway is a door or connection between one section of your environment and another. A typical company has multiple connections between the Internet and the extranet of its enterprise, and you can refer to each as a gateway.

You should deploy certain products at the gateway to protect your enterprise, the most important being a firewall. A firewall prevents unauthorized information, commonly referred to as *traffic*, from passing into or out of your gateway.

Another important gateway product is anti-virus software, particularly on your email gateway. Anti-virus software at the gateway is important because it protects your environment from viruses before they can enter.

You can use content filtering to control unwanted email, commonly known as *spam*, and to *filter* (restrict) access to certain Internet addresses that your company might deem inappropriate. Common restrictions include pornography, hate, and gambling web sites.

Gateway products are your first line of defense for protecting your company from threats, such as computer viruses, before they get inside your network.

Server

Servers are shared computers that perform functions for multiple personnel at a company, such as storing files or running a shared application, including ERP or CRM. Put simply, *servers* provide *services*. Your second line of defense is at the server level, and you should ensure that many or all of your servers have protection on them.

Protection for a given server should vary according to its role in your business. Departmental servers used for storing files and printing usually do not require as much protection as e-commerce servers, and you might decide that scanning these servers for any known vulnerabilities on a regular basis is protection enough.

On the other hand, you should definitely be concerned about protecting mission-critical servers or any other key servers within the company. These servers should have anti-virus protection, especially if they're Windows-based, because Windows has the greatest exposure to viruses. You should install host-based intrusion detection and vulnerability management protection and ensure that you also protect those servers with network-based intrusion detection and vulnerability management tools.

Multiple *clients* use servers. If a virus or worm infects a server, it can also infect all the clients that rely upon that server. This can have a ripple effect across your organization, causing widespread outages that affect your business. This was the case with the blended threats Code Red and Nimda.

It's important to classify your servers according to business need because the investment required to deploy security products on each of these servers can be cost prohibitive.

Client

The third layer is the individual *client* systems that each employee uses, including laptops, desktops, and digital assistants (PDAs). Portable clients are challenging from a security perspective because when an employee leaves the office, he or she loses the protection of your company's security systems, which means that you must install a subset of the entire security solution on each portable client.

It's important to provide anti-virus protection to portable clients to prevent them from infecting other clients when they return to your office and connect to your network. Anti-virus solutions have addressed this issue, and you can use them to distribute virus definitions to local and remote staff automatically and to scan laptop computers when they return to the office.

The major challenge is often that every employee has one or multiple computers that need protection. Automated solutions are available that remotely distribute security tools and prevent employees from inadvertently turning them off. Although automated tools can help, diligence is required because a single client has the potential to create widespread problems for your business.

Special Considerations—Wireless and PDAs

Wireless computing and the proliferation of PDAs pose unique challenges to your information security program. Wireless technology has liberated computer users, enabling them to connect to their networks while roaming instead of having a network cable tether them in one location; this trend will continue to grow into the future. However, because this technology was first developed for nonbusiness consumers, higher priorities were placed on ease of use instead of security. Thus, wireless devices do not always use encryption when transmitting data, and when they do, the technology is often ineffective.

Authentication, or the ability to determine who is trying to access systems, is also limited with wireless technology and does not scale to the enterprise level. It's also easy for someone to plug an unauthorized wireless device into your corporate network and immediately open a *hole* in your computing environment that an unauthorized user can use to gain access to your company's resources.

PDAs pose threats similar to wireless technology. Because of their small form factor, PDAs are easily lost or stolen. This is a major security issue today because more people are using these devices to store business information, and virtually no security exists within PDAs today. Often, even if a PDA has password authentication, a hacker can bypass it easily. PDA users almost never encrypt their data, and anyone who gains access to the device can read all the stored information. Therefore, although storing customer contact information on one of these devices can appear harmless, the loss of a device could result in major embarrassment to your company.

You should carefully manage these devices in your environment and establish policies to restrict their usage because you will not have the technical enforcement mechanisms to protect your computing environment. Treat wireless devices as critical assets that your staff needs to manage; it is quite easy to consider them only as personal productivity tools and lose track of how people might use them within your company.

Decisions/Alternatives to Consider

When you are setting up the technology component of your information security program, you must make some key decisions. We will cover two of these decisions in this section. The first is deciding whether to use a best of breed solution from multiple vendors as opposed to an integrated solution from a single vendor. The second decision is whether to implement software products that are installed on your servers or to rely upon security appliances.

Best of Breed and Integrated Solutions

The decision to use multiple vendors that each offer the best product in a given category versus a single vendor that can offer a complete suite of solutions is a debate that extends far beyond information security.

You might want to choose a firewall from one vendor, anti-virus from a second, and intrusion detection software from a third. This is referred to as a *best of breed* solution because you are using multiple vendors, each providing the best solution for a particular security need. On the other hand, you might want an *integrated solution* from a single vendor that offers all three products. An integrated solution can also be best of breed depending on the products, vendor, and solution.

The challenge that this poses to your information technology organization is that they need to do the integration work to make products from multiple vendors work together. Best of breed vendors are constantly trying to extend their product lines to address additional portions of the market, so these companies don't place a high priority on ensuring interoperability with other vendors' products.

Vendors that offer a complete suite of products spend more time ensuring interoperability between their product suites. These vendors reduce the IT burden of integrating products from multiple sources, which can be difficult when relying upon multiple vendors. Best practices in this area include relying upon as few vendors as possible; a single vendor for your information security products is ideal. If you can find a vendor that offers an integrated solution with good functionality, it will greatly simplify your environment and increase your likelihood of success.

Server-Based Solutions Versus Appliances

The emergence of security appliances has created an alternative to the traditional method of installing and maintaining all the various security software products on your own servers. Appliances are hardware devices that also include traditional security software. The work that was formerly required to install and configure software on a server-by-server basis is no longer necessary. You can preconfigure these appliances and ship them to remote offices for installation by nontechnical staff. This approach reduces the burden of having your staff travel to each office to install or support security products.

The fuller functionality offered by the more traditional software-based products offsets this convenience. Software products are often more scalable and provide more features than you will find on an appliance. However, the gap between appliances and server-based solutions will close over time as information security organizations need to protect more of their computing environments and require simpler solutions with less administrative overhead. The best practice in this area is to simplify your environment and deploy as few individual solutions as possible.

Business Models

Your technology program also needs to be able to support your current and planned business models. This might include your company's desire to conduct more of its business electronically using an e-commerce site. The technology strategy for this environment will be different from one that only uses the Internet for a simple web site that contains company information. You need to back up business decisions to offer products and services electronically by conducting a thorough risk analysis of alternative information security programs.

Other examples include supply chain management and the need to connect with your customers and partners electronically. This can range from electronic exchange of files such as electronic data interchange (EDI) to allowing customers and partners to directly access your network. These business models require considerable analysis and planning to ensure that you protect the assets of your company, your business partners, and your customers. Your information security organization should be included during planning for these products and service offerings to avoid costly delays or embarrassments later.

Technology—Components

At this point, you should have a better idea of the technology products that exist and how they can be used together to provide multiple layers of protection. The question we need to answer is, "How do I get started, and what are some of the best practices in this area?" Figure 6-3 provides an overview of the hierarchy for implementing security technology.

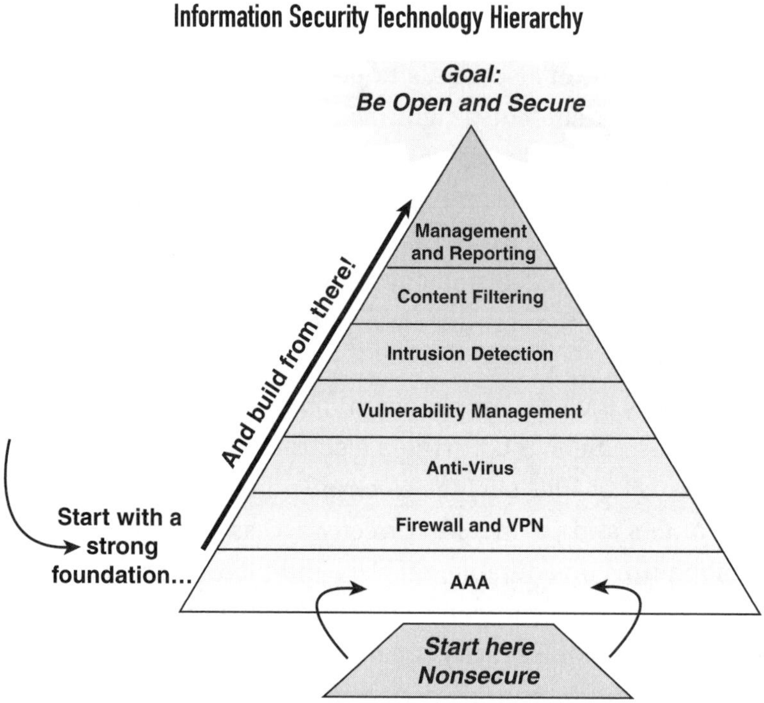

Information Security Technology Hierarchy

Goal:
Be Open and Secure

Management and Reporting

Content Filtering

Intrusion Detection

Vulnerability Management

Anti-Virus

Firewall and VPN

AAA

And build from there!

Start with a strong foundation...

Start here Nonsecure

Figure 6-3 Technology hierarchy of security.

This hierarchy presents the relative priority for implementing each of these technologies at your company. You can use this hierarchy to help determine the priority for deploying products in your environment and to assist in determining which additional products to deploy in the future.

At the basic level, you should be addressing the AAA portion of your program by ensuring that user IDs and passwords are required to access your systems. You can build upon this foundation until you are implementing tools that are more sophisticated. This is a simplistic view of technology, but it gives you an idea of where to start.

Industry best practices for information security technology describe how you should leverage a combination of available technologies to protect your enterprise. Several sources are available for industry best practices; include Visa's *"Digital Dozen,"* which outlines the requirements that you must meet to use their service. Appendix B, "Information Security Web Sites," contains several web sites that you can use to find out more about these practices and how you can implement them at your company.

Security Technology Categories

Several categories of information security products are available to protect your company. These categories range from basic AAA technology (user IDs and passwords) to management products for some or all of your security tools. Table 6-2 provides a summary of the major security technologies available to protect your enterprise and a brief description of their capabilities.

Table 6-2

Information Security Technology Categories

Technology	Category	Description
■ Authentication, authorization and accounting (AAA)	■ User IDs and passwords ■ Electronic or physical keys ■ Biometrics ■ Remote access	■ Used to limit access to resources to authorized users only. ■ Technology ranges from simple user IDs and passwords to more sophisticated biometrics.
■ Firewalls/VPN	■ Packet filtering ■ Stateful inspection ■ Proxy-based ■ VPN	■ Looks at "header" or beginning of each message to determine whether the message is okay. ■ Reviews traffic in a "state table" to monitor for security violations. ■ Reads and rewrites each message to ensure that messages are valid. ■ Used for secure remote access over a public network (such as the Internet).
■ Anti-virus	■ Gateway ■ Server ■ Client	■ Two methods for addressing viruses: ■ Signature recognition of virus that is known in advance, such as the name in the subject line of an email. ■ Heuristics to find patterns and conditions that identify a virus.

continues

Technology	Category	Description
■ Vulnerability management	■ Network-based	■ Automated tools that rely upon databases of known vulnerabilities to proactively review (scan) for vulnerabilities.
	■ Host-based	■ Vulnerability examples include security patches that have been released by vendors and need to be applied, or certain system default settings that should be updated.
		■ These tools can be installed to protect a specific server in the case of host-based or can reside on a single server and scan the network in the case of network-based.
■ Intrusion detection	■ Network-based	■ Reactive tools that set off "alarms" when unauthorized activities occur in environment.
	■ Host-based	■ These tools can also be network or host-based in the same manner as vulnerability management.
■ Content filtering	■ Email ■ Web	■ Allow companies to restrict access or filter email and access to web.
		■ Spam control is the most common type of email filtering.
		■ Restricted access to porn sites is the most frequently used type of web filtering.
■ Security management and reporting	■ Device	■ Management of a single tool such as a firewall is the basic form of management, followed by managing multiple tools.
	■ Multi-device	■ Multi-device management includes the management of different devices or vendors.

continues

Technology	Category	Description
	■ Correlation	■ Correlation includes gathering information from all the devices in your network and identifying patterns that might require further investigation.
	■ Visualization	■ Visualization provides graphical representation of data for easy identification of issues.
■ Encryption	■ Symmetric	■ Same key used to encrypt and decrypt messages.
	■ Asymmetric	■ Different keys used for encrypting and decrypting messages.
■ Appliances	■ Multifunction	■ Appliances are hardware devices that combine some or all of the security technology in a single unit.
		■ Appliances are intended to be configured by security staff centrally and installed by nontechnical staff.

Practical Deployment of Technology

This section reviews some of the trade-offs that you will face when deploying security technology and offers some suggestions. Each major category of product is presented along with examples that give a better understanding of how you can use the product to form an effective program.

Authentication, Authorization, and Accounting (AAA)

AAA is an important element of your program because it enables you to establish the identity of individuals and then determine whether you have authorized them to access a particular asset or network. During accounting, AAA provides auditing of which personnel are using particular resources at your company.

AAA is also important when determining who has access in a specific location and across the enterprise. An employee might have broad access to systems at headquarters but little or no access to systems from a remote location. It's important to have a combination of AAA security in place to enable employees to get their jobs completed while ensuring that only authorized staff can access sensitive information.

Identity management includes all the components of AAA, with the addition of *provisioning* to manage the deployment of accounts and *directory services* to manage their usage. The objective is to have a source of information within the company that identifies all staff members and the systems they are able to access. This is particularly important in larger companies with multiple systems that employees need to access on a daily basis. For example, at a large software company in Silicon Valley, a newly hired security manager discovered that there were 30% more active remote access accounts than there were personnel at the company at that time. This included employees who had left the company more than three years before. In another example, a disgruntled individual remotely accessed the network of his former employer (a billion-dollar global company) and maliciously deleted critical applications, causing damage to the company and taking down its business systems for 48 hours. This individual was convicted in December 2003, sentenced to federal prison for one year, and ordered to pay restitution.

An important objective for *identity management* is to provide *single sign-on,* or a single user ID and password that your employees can use to access authorized systems. However, most companies have not achieved this objective.

Although each security product relies upon a similar set of protocols for authentication, vendors have not worked together to integrate their products. The industry is giving considerable attention to this area, and viable solutions will be forthcoming.

Authentication

How do you determine that somebody is actually who they say they are? Obviously, this is necessary to control access to systems. As we introduced in Chapter 2, "Information Security Overview," authentication is the process that verifies the identity of a user so that you can grant or deny access to protected resources.

Authentication techniques range from a simple login based upon user IDs and passwords to more powerful mechanisms such as tokens, public-key certificates, and biometrics. The industry refers to the different authentication methods as *factors*. These factors are as follows:

- **First factor**—Something you know
- **Second factor**—Something you have
- **Third factor**—Something you are
- **Fourth factor**—Where you are

First Factor

The first factor is *something you know*. The most common form of authentication is a user name and password combination. Unfortunately, hackers can often guess user names because most companies use one of three common naming formats (that is, the first initial of the first name followed by the last name, firstname.lastname, or firstname_lastname). This means that hackers already have half of what they need to log on to someone's account. The other half is a password, which is notorious for being weak. Staff often use default passwords on accounts, set their passwords to the word *password*, or choose a spouse's name or other words that a hacker can guess easily.

Second Factor

A second factor is *something you have,* in addition to something that you know, such as an ATM card. However, ATM cards are easily lost or stolen, and if someone guesses your PIN, he will be able to access your account.

A *token* is another example of second factor authentication. A token can be *hard,* such as a security identification card, or *soft,* such as software tokens installed on a particular laptop that you can't transfer to someone else. To gain access, you must have that particular laptop and know the password that unlocks the token. When a staff member uses this laptop remotely, you should require another password to access the company's network.

You should also require second factor authentication to get logical access to mission-critical systems and remote access into a network because user names and passwords are not good enough. A second factor provides a balance of security and ease of use.

Third Factor

The third factor is *something you are*. Technology to determine who you are has been around for some time. Professionals call it *biometric authentication*, but it's only just beginning to become widespread. Organizations often use biometric authentication to restrict access to data centers. Common examples of biometric authentication include the following:

- Fingerprints
- Hand geometry
- Retina scan
- Iris scan

Fingerprint scans are widely used, whereas the retina and iris scans are rare. Many people find that having a light shone into their eyes is quite uncomfortable. The United States Citizenship and Immigration Services (formally Immigration and Naturalization Services or INS) uses biometric authentication based upon hand geometry, whereas the U.S. Customs Service uses biometric fingerprint readers to screen visitors who enter the country.

The problem with biometric access is that you have to ensure uniqueness, and only certain types of body measurements are unique. Although fingerprints are widely accepted, hackers can forge them. Retinal scans, although not widely used due to comfort level and their adaptability to different security applications, are the safest and guarantee uniqueness.

Fourth Factor

The fourth factor is *where you are*; however, this technique is not widely accepted and might not be for several years. This factor uses the Global Positioning System (GPS) to pinpoint the location of an individual, followed by determining if you have authorized that individual to be at that location. The fourth factor should never be used solely; however, you can use it in conjunction with the second or third factors.

Authentication Protocols

Authentication systems use *protocols* for authentication to evaluate messages and determine whether they are appropriate. Protocols are rules based upon established standards, which you can use to determine whether a message conforms to established guidelines and can be considered authentic. Three protocols that exist for authentication include Kerberos, RADIUS, and 802.1x:

- **Kerberos**—A security system developed at MIT that authenticates users. It does not provide authorization to services or databases; it establishes identity at logon for use throughout the session. Vendors embed this technology in products such as Novell NetWare and Microsoft Windows. Additional systems such as the company's email system would also leverage this technology and require another user ID and password to access that system.

- **RADIUS** (**R**emote **A**uthentication **D**ial-**I**n **U**ser **S**ervice)—An authentication protocol that uses a challenge/response method of authentication for remote users. For staff members who travel or work from home, you ideally want to identify the computer they are using, in addition to requiring a user ID and password, because simple user IDs and passwords can easily be compromised, and the potential for unauthorized access is significant.

- **802.1x**—A security protocol from the IEEE for wired networks and wireless local area networks that adheres to the 802.11 standard. It relies on the Extensible Authentication Protocol (EAP) to pass messages to any of a variety of authentication servers such as RADIUS or Kerberos.

Authorization

Now that you've determined who this individual is, does he have authorization to access your systems? Authorization is the process of ensuring that an individual has access to only the information that he needs but not more.

Another important concept enforced through authorization is the separation of duties. For example, within the finance organization, a staff member should not be able to enter a purchase order and then approve the payment. Otherwise, this individual has the ability to commit fraud by setting up a vendor's purchase order and then approving payment to that vendor.

You should set up authorization in user groups based upon roles within an organization, not specific individuals. You can set up groups for functional areas such as accounts payable and purchasing and give certain staff in these groups additional levels of authority based upon their responsibility. This is especially important in larger companies because identifying the appropriate access for each department is time-consuming, and it is much easier to place an employee in a group instead of creating a custom account for each employee.

Privileged, or *administrative*, access to systems needs to be carefully controlled. Staff with this authorization can perform all functions on the system. In the case of an email system, this staff person can not only set up and delete accounts but also read everyone's email, which is something that needs to be restricted to a small number of staff.

Accounting

Accounting, the third element of AAA, serves the dual purpose of audit and resource usage. From an audit perspective, it is important to have a good understanding of who is accessing the various resources within the company and get specific details on what these people are doing. It's a good practice to review logs of restricted systems to ensure that only authorized individuals are accessing them. In addition, a regular review of employees who have access to restricted areas, such as the company's data center, is a good idea.

On a periodic basis, you should also review the frequency, duration, actual functions performed, and time that someone accesses systems to identify inappropriate patterns. You might have authorized an employee to access the company's payroll system; however, using this system during nonbusiness hours when his supervisor is not around might be an issue.

Resource usage is the second element of accounting, and you can use it to allocate costs between various departments based upon their actual usage. Companies that follow resource charge-back models can leverage these accounting capabilities to identify usage by individuals for this purpose. This was more popular with time-sharing systems and is not very prevalent today. Accounting and auditing are reactive enforcement mechanisms to ensure that your staff is properly enforcing authentication and authorization.

Identity Management

AAA has been a huge problem for enterprises because you have to perform all three functions on a system-by-system or application-by-application basis. If you authenticate someone for application A, you must authenticate him again for application B. You also must set up the privilege levels or authorization for that user for each application.

Account administration is a huge, labor-intensive process. Every time you set up an account, you are also risking the possibility of introducing errors into the process. Those errors can be relatively simple; for example, is Joe Smith the same as Joseph Smith or Joseph A. Smith? How do you know which person you've been talking about? Every time you set up authorization, there are always potential risks for human error.

In recent years, a solution commonly called identity management has come to the forefront of AAA. Identity management is an attempt to standardize the AAA process across the environment. The goal is to ensure that authentication and authorization of various applications is being performed in a single location and to centralize accounting.

Identity management not only encompasses AAA but also addresses provisioning and directory services. Figure 6-4 provides a graphic overview of identity management.

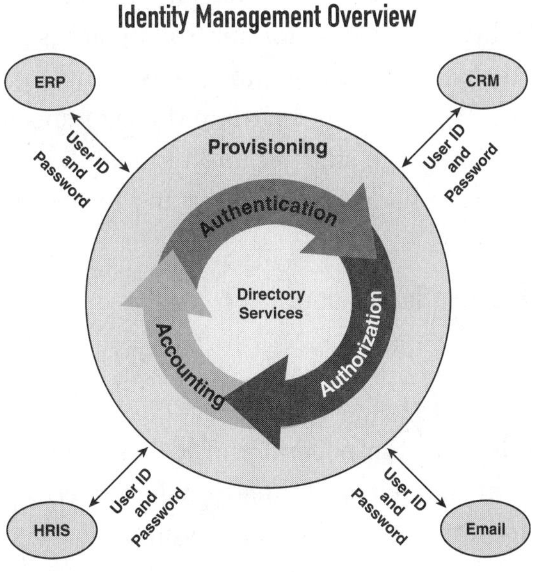

Identity Management Overview

Figure 6-4 Identity management.

As we mentioned earlier, the two key extensions to AAA include *provisioning* to manage the overall account management process and *directory services* to house all this information. Account provisioning includes the creation, management, and deletion of accounts for individuals as they come into an enterprise, or more importantly from a security perspective, when they leave or are terminated. You must ensure that you close all accounts belonging to former employees promptly so that they don't have unauthorized access to the systems, especially in the case of disgruntled employees. The goal is to automate many of these processes to speed up the handling of requests and eliminate the possibility of human error.

All of the relevant people information comes from the human resources system and is housed in one directory that serves as the ultimate source of information for staff and the systems it is authorized to use. This simplifies the process because this information access is no longer required on multiple systems. Identity management is part of an attempt to do away with the AAA nightmare.

Single sign-on takes this one step further and provides one user ID and password to access all the systems for the company. As mentioned previously, the more user IDs that an employee has to deal with, the less likely he is to keep this information more secure.

The extension of AAA to identity management and the availability of single sign-on will simplify the process for controlling access to systems. These solutions make it much easier for users to create a single password that follows security best practices such as length and use of special characters. These solutions also reduce the staff required to maintain all these accounts and ensure that your team handles new hires and terminations quickly.

Information Security Program Technology

Firewalls

Firewalls are one of the most important and widely deployed security tools. Before deploying them yourself, you must consider *internal* versus *external deployment* and restrictions on services and protocols.

If you install a firewall at the gateway to protect the DMZ, this is an external deployment because it is outside of the interior zone of your computing environment. The firewalls that separate the general production network, or interior zone, from the mission-critical zone are *interior deployments.*

Next, you must decide which services and protocols you will permit to flow between firewalls and create an *allow list.* It's better to determine which types of traffic you are willing to allow because this will be a much shorter list than what you are not willing to allow. The default setting on your firewall should be *deny,* blocking all traffic that is not on the allow list.

Your allow list will vary depending on the portion of your environment that you are protecting. In general, the closer you get to the mission-critical zone, the smaller your allow list, because only the essential services and protocols are permitted in this zone.

Several types of firewalls are available today, and the best way to describe them is by comparing them against the Open Systems Interconnection (OSI) reference model. The OSI reference model is a worldwide standard that defines a framework for implementing communications protocols in seven layers. In the OSI model, data passes from one layer to the next, starting at the application layer and proceeding to the bottom layer, before passing back up the hierarchy at its destination.

The various types of firewalls operate at different layers that provide varying levels of security. Figure 6-5 provides a graphic view of the OSI model and the major categories of firewalls.

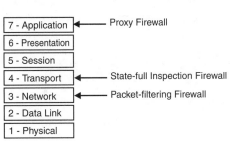

Figure 6-5 OSI model and firewalls.

The higher you get on the OSI model, the more secure the firewall, but the slower the performance because they migrate from packet filtering to proxy firewalls.

Firewalls are relatively new and are security-specific devices. A few years ago, firewalls did not exist, and network devices called *routers* performed their security functions. You can configure a router to do packet filtering, which includes inspection of the header of a message (but not the payload) to determine any issues. Routers can also filter certain traffic based upon their Internet Protocol (IP) address. However, the role of routers is to route traffic and provide connectivity, whereas firewalls do the opposite—they deny or block connectivity. The best practice is not to use a router as a firewall.

Packet filtering and statefull inspection firewalls are quite fast in terms of the throughput that they are able to handle. However, packet filtering only inspects the headers of data packets, not the payload, which means that packet filtering firewalls are fast but not as secure as another type of firewall, the proxy firewall.

Proxy firewalls look at headers but also take the individual packets as they come in and rewrite them to ensure that they are in the proper format. These firewalls filter out any attacks, many buffer overflows, and things that aren't in compliance with the Request for Comments (RFC). RFCs are documents used by the Internet Engineering Task Force (IETF) to define specifications for a particular technology—in this case, TCP/IP communications. No direct connection exists between the outside world and the inside world during this process.

Unfortunately, because they do more work, proxy firewalls are slower. The bandwidth they can handle is less than a statefull inspection firewall. If you have a high-volume site or server that does not contain mission-critical information, it's probably acceptable to use the statefull inspection firewall rather than the proxy firewall. If you have a lower bandwidth site, but the data is much more sensitive, a proxy firewall would be more appropriate.

Almost all proxy firewalls also have the capability to act as statefull inspection firewalls for specific connections. Thus, it's not an either-or situation with a proxy firewall; you can choose between proxy and packet filtering where necessary. However, packet-filtering firewalls cannot operate as proxy firewalls.

Anti-Virus

Anti-virus software is a required part of any security program. Approximately 65,000 viruses for Windows-based systems exist, and virus writers create more on a daily basis. Far fewer viruses infect UNIX systems, and an even smaller number of viruses exist for Linux. Virus writers like to target Windows because it is the prevalent operating system worldwide. However, virus problems will continue to worsen for UNIX and Linux because their increasing popularity makes them an attractive target.

It's important to keep virus definitions up-to-date so that your anti-virus software can identify and eliminate new viruses. In the past, updating virus definitions relied on people, and people don't update their virus definitions very often. They tend to install the software and forget about it, so having software that can update these definitions automatically is extremely important.

Two other key requirements include having the ability to enforce these updates within the enterprise and the ability to check for infected systems automatically. Fortunately, all these capabilities are now standard offerings from commercially available anti-virus solutions. Best practices call for a regular schedule to scan all systems in your environment on a weekly basis and to update definitions on a daily basis.

Traditional anti-virus products only looked at email or Simple Mail Transfer Protocol (SMTP). However, malware can now spread in several different ways, including Hypertext Transfer Protocol (HTTP) and File Transfer Protocol (FTP), which are used by Internet browsers when accessing the web. In addition, users can spread viruses through the file transfer capabilities included in many instant messaging programs.

Having anti-virus products at the gateway to scan multiple protocols or services is important because hackers can use these various methods to transfer malicious software. Anti-virus software must remain a key component of your information security program because the threats of infection are increasing.

Vulnerability Management

As we discussed in Chapter 2, *Vulnerability Management* (VM) can be host-based, meaning it runs directly on the system that it's checking for vulnerabilities, or it can be network-based. Network-based VM can scan the network, looking at many different servers and clients to identify possible vulnerabilities.

Host-based VM provides an inside-out view of how effectively things are running on that system, so it's a much more accurate view of how your staff has configured that system. Some of the questions that host-based VM can answer about a system include the following:

- Has it been properly hardened from the operating system perspective?
- Have the applications been hardened?
- Have unnecessary services been removed?
- Have appropriate patches been applied?

Host-based VM requires more time for installation, more data to review, and more licenses, all of which results in a higher cost than network-based VM. This will probably limit your deployment of host-based VM to a subset of the total server population. The most important servers are the externally facing and mission-critical systems, so these generally need host-based VM.

From a time (and cost) perspective, it's easier to use network-based VM. The tool can reside on a single server and scan other servers and clients on your network. Network-based VM provides a view from the outside in. It does not give you the current patch level, and it can't tell you exactly how the system has been hardened, but it can tell you if your staff has missed any vulnerability or patches. Nonetheless, network-based VM is faster and easier to conduct and therefore is less expensive than host-based vulnerability management.

Having a good backup and recovery program is another proactive element to your information security program. Critical information should be backed up on a regular basis to ensure that you can re-create this information, should it become unavailable. These backups should be carefully planned to address critical business time frames such as year-end processing. Backup tapes should be stored in a separate location and verified on a regular basis to ensure that they are working correctly.

Intrusion Detection

Like vulnerability management tools, *Intrusion Detection Systems* (IDSs) can be both host- and network-based. Host-based IDSs require that an agent be running on every server or system that you want to protect.

A host-based system can tell you specifically when an intruder has compromised a host. However, it cannot tell you if the intruder also compromised the server right next door. Although it provides you with a definitive view of a single host, it cannot provide the bigger picture.

For this, you must turn to a network-based IDS. It can tell you that a hacker is attacking server 1, server 2, and server 3 and the specific type of attack on each system. However, a network-based IDS has no idea if those attacks were successful. It saw the bad traffic go by and knows where it was going, but it can't tell you what happened after it got there.

For this reason, you should deploy both host- and network-based IDS. Used together, host- and network-based IDS gives you the complete view of what the attack looks like across your network and how successful that attack was.

IDS systems do not do anything to prevent an attack. IDS informs you, in a timely manner, of the fact that you have a problem on your network As a best practice, always use vulnerability management combined with IDS and augment host-based systems with network-based tools. Vulnerability management alone isn't sufficient protection for external-facing, mission-critical systems.

Security Management

Another major gap exists with security management. Most organizations today deploy a wide range of products from multiple vendors to address their security needs. For example, a small company of approximately 1,000 employees could easily have deployed the following information security tools to address its basic requirements:

- 5 or more firewalls
- 25 or more host-based intrusion detection devices
- 2 or more network-based intrusion detection devices

- An equal number of host- and network-based vulnerability management tools to complement the intrusion detection devices

- Anti-virus on all external gateways (5), key servers (25), and all clients (1,000)

These products probably came from multiple vendors. The challenge from an information security perspective is that your staff must manage each product. The vendors might provide a console to manage their own products, but this won't assist your staff when managing another vendor's products.

The ideal scenario would be to have a single management console that takes care of all the devices that are deployed at the company. This scenario would also have a single management console that takes care of all your security devices, but in reality, you might end up with a large number of management consoles.

Information Overload

Information overload is a major issue for information security organizations. Security devices produce large amounts of data, and when you aggregate this data across the enterprise, it's too much for a human to handle alone. To find critical information that you can use to make decisions, you must sift through too much information.

Data is collected at three different levels: *events*, *alerts*, and *incidents*. The first level, *events*, involves what a system is doing. Windows and UNIX generate systems logs, which contain raw events that tell you exactly what the systems are doing. These logs produce a huge amount of technical information that you can use for forensic purposes. Therefore, logging the day-to-day events is important, but it's not something that you want to review on a regular basis.

Alerts are the second level of data generated by your security systems. Examples include repeated failed user authentication or a firewall closing certain ports in reaction to a possible attack. It's important to be able to track all the alerts and send them to a central management console for review.

Events and alerts provide a technical perspective of what happened, but this isn't enough to base your decisions on. The *events* log everything, good and bad, while your systems generate *alerts* when events reach certain thresholds, such as after the third time that someone enters the wrong password. In this case, the account is disabled, and the system generates an alert to notify the support staff of this situation. If the user successfully logs into the system after entering his password twice, the system logs the events but doesn't generate an alert.

You can't react to all the alerts in a given day, so you need to correlate these into *incidents* to discern patterns. Incidents are your third level of data; you need to investigate incidents further on a management level.

If you have an unusually large number of alerts of users entering their passwords incorrectly, this might be a hacker trying to break into one of your systems by guessing passwords. This is an incident, and in this case, one of your information security staff needs to investigate. Figure 6-6 provides a graphic view of this issue and the staff using the different levels of data.

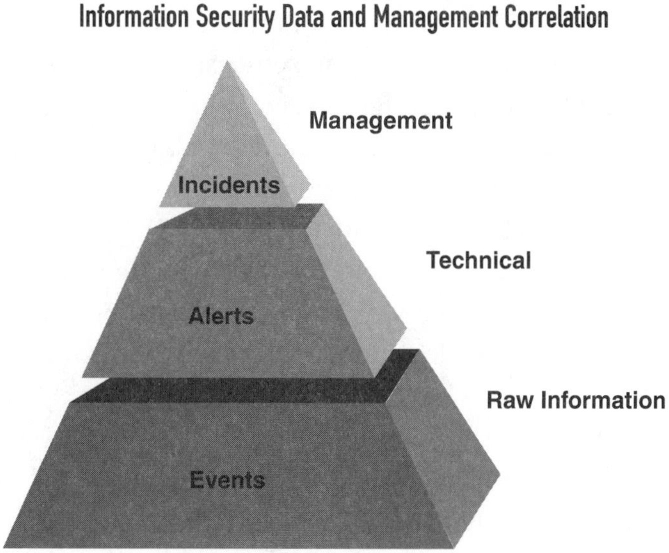

Information Security Data and Management Correlation

Figure 6-6 Correlations between information and management.

Data Analysis

Referring back to our previous example, you will probably have multiple security devices from more than one vendor. All these devices create logs and alerts that your information security staff needs to sift through to identify any security issues within your organization. The major steps in this process are as follows:

- Common logging, reporting, and alerting
- Normalization
- Correlation
- Visualization

Common logging, reporting, and alerting include capturing information from all these devices (aggregation of data). *Normalization* transfers all this information into a common format. This is a critical step because no common reporting standards exist today; each vendor generates information in its own unique format.

Correlation follows normalization and is an evaluation of these logs or alerts to identify patterns that might represent issues in your environment. Certain attacks follow a known pattern based upon the steps that a hacker must follow to exploit a specific weakness and break into your systems. During correlation, you can discover these patterns and determine if an intruder has compromised your security.

The final step is *visualization;* this includes generating summary graphs that identify these attacks so that your staff can react appropriately. Wading through volumes of text-based logs and alert messages is not a user-friendly experience, so visualization is key to helping your staff quickly understand and react to incidents.

To put all this information in perspective, refer to Figure 6-7 for a representation of the amount of information that a security manager from a medium-sized company needs to work with in a given month.

A Month in the Life of an IT Security Manager

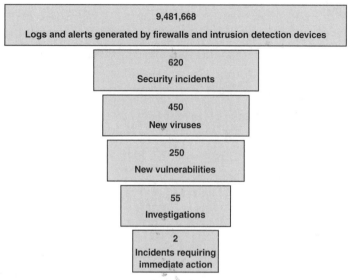

Source: Symantec

Figure 6-7   A month in the life of an IT security manager.

At the minimum, a manager needs to be able to aggregate and normalize all the data to manage all the individual security products. Your information security staff doesn't want raw data—it wants the analysis applied against the raw information, and it wants intelligence. Text alone is not as effective as a visual representation of the situation.

Solutions are necessary to manage this data overload so that you and your staff can focus on resolving incidents, not sifting through data. Early versions of products are available today, although this is an immature area of information security, and these early solutions need significant improvement.

Remember, a single tool will not protect your environment, so you must determine the appropriate combination of tools that offer you optimal protection. Proactive management and data analysis will enable your team to focus its attention where it will do the greatest good for your security program.

Security Forensics

Forensics is a narrow security area that is not a high priority for most organizations, due to the unique tools and specialized staff required. It is better to leverage a company that focuses on this area, should your organization need to collect evidence for a criminal investigation. These companies are familiar with the process for legal investigation, collecting evidence, and preparing this evidence for prosecution. The laws in this area change frequently, and your in-house security staff can better spend its time on other areas outlined in this book. Resources found in Appendix B can be used to identify qualified organizations to help in this area.

Technology—Administration

Deploying these solutions is just the first step. A proactive regimen of scanning and remediation, strengthened by independent evaluation of your program, is an important part of securing your information systems. In addition, you must be able to demonstrate that you are making progress, and to do this, you need *metrics* in place to measure improvement in your processes.

Scanning and Remediation

As we discussed in Chapter 5, "Process," a regular program of scanning your environment to identify and address vulnerabilities is quite important. Tools are available to help your organization prioritize the remediation effort.

Using these tools, you can classify your vulnerabilities into high, medium, and low priorities. You should also classify your assets according to criticality and focus your remediation effort on the critical and mission-critical areas of your enterprise.

Securing vulnerabilities in your systems, or *remediation,* is a labor-intensive process that includes two processes: *hardening* and *patching.* Hardening addresses securing vulnerabilities resulting from default or incorrect system configurations. Computer manufacturers often ship their products in a usable, but insecure configuration because they want to minimize technical support calls. Their expectation is that after you become familiar with the product, you will be in a much better position to choose the available options, including security. A product might have many security features available; however, in the default configuration, the vendor has disabled these features because they place too many restrictions on use and require considerable time to configure. In addition, systems often ship with default passwords that hackers know, no password at all, or a password of "password." These default password settings are an example of a vulnerability that your organization will address through hardening, hopefully before you start using a new product. Hardening generally takes the opposite approach of vendors and disables anything that you don't require in your environment. Your staff can find guidelines for hardening different areas of your environment, such as hardware or operating systems, on the Internet.

Patching, on the other hand, is the process of applying *vendor-provided* fixes that address stability and security problems with specific products. Patching is labor-intensive because vendors release new patches on a daily basis, and your staff must test each patch prior to deploying it enterprise-wide.

Automated solutions for patching haven't been very successful, and you should not consider using one without adequate testing beforehand. In the future, these solutions might work in simple environments; however, it's unlikely that you will ever be able to address complex systems (such as ERP) in this manner. In the meantime, a regular program of scanning and remediation is an important component of your information security program.

Independent Program Review

An independent review of your information security program is something that you should consider. Public companies have been undergoing independent audits of their financial controls for years; this serves to validate that management is doing its job properly. An independent security review is no different, and it is an excellent way for you to gauge the effectiveness of your program.

Two examples of independent reviews include penetration testing and formal auditing. Penetration testing involves hiring a third party to attempt to break into your company's business systems. Using the same tools that a hacker would, these individuals try to bypass your security program and gain unauthorized access to your systems, identifying weaknesses in your processes. Due to the dynamic nature of the information security field, it is recommended that you conduct these tests at least annually.

Formal audits of your information security program are an effective means of identifying areas for improvement. The scope and focus of these audits will vary over time. It's important to explain to your staff that this is not a "witch hunt" but rather an ongoing process to ensure that the necessary controls are in place.

Hold kick-off meetings with staff affected by the audit to review the overall scope and their roles in the process. Circulate the results of the audit to affected parties to develop remediation plans. It is important to track the results of audits over time to ensure that your team makes progress and that the same issues do not appear in successive audits. Because audits are more time-consuming and expensive than penetration testing, auditing annually is sufficient for most enterprises.

Anti-Virus Update Program

To remain effective, anti-virus solutions require new virus definitions each time a new virus appears, which can occur daily. This requires your company to update these definitions to ensure that you remain protected. Anti-virus is a mature area of the information security industry, and solutions are available to automatically distribute these definitions throughout your company. You can configure these solutions to perform several key activities, including distribution of definitions, regular scanning, and support of traveling employees.

Best practices for updating anti-virus software include these:

- Updating your definitions on a daily basis due to the large number of new viruses. A common practice is to schedule these activities during off hours for desktop computers and the first time portable computers log into the network each day.

- Scanning your computer for known viruses on a weekly basis. Viruses and worms have numerous methods for spreading and can easily infect your computer.

- Updating definitions for traveling employees before you allow them to access systems remotely.

It only takes one unprotected computer to spread a virus or other malicious content within your company. Every person who accesses your computer systems, including employees, contractors, and temporary staff, needs to have anti-virus software installed on his computer.

Program Measurement

It's likely that you're devoting significant resources to the technology component of your program. To ensure that your information security program is improving over time, it is important to put together a set of metrics to monitor your progress. Your metrics might start out basic, such as measuring the number of security incidents in a given month, and grow with your system.

Unfortunately, the information security industry does not have a standard set of metrics such as sales growth, earnings per share, and profitability, which business people commonly use to measure the financial health of a company. Information security metrics generally focus on how your program might have prevented something bad from happening at your company.

For example, the capability of your program to detect and prevent attacks would be a useful metric. Table 6-3 outlines sample metrics that you might consider for your company's program.

Table 6-3

High-Level Information Security Metrics	
Category	**Security Metric**
Measuring security policy compliance	■ Percentage of company that is following established policies such as proper passwords ■ Number of policy exemptions granted in a given month
Measuring security awareness	■ Percentage of information technology staff that is aware of security policies ■ Percentage of users who are aware of security policies ■ Percentage of employees with security responsibility who have received training within the past year
Measuring risk	■ Number of "holes" found by vulnerability scans ■ Percentage of attacks detected during penetration test ■ Percentage of systems with documented risk assessments ■ Percentage of systems that have Business Continuity Plans ■ Percentage of systems that have tested Business Continuity Plans over past year
Measuring response	■ Percentage of attempted attacks that were successful ■ Mean time to threat identification ■ Mean time to threat resolution

Identify assets that are critical to your company and align your metrics to measure your success in protecting them. In the case of a software company, your most valuable asset is the source code for your products. Metrics to evaluate how well you have protected these assets from unauthorized access are most useful when demonstrating the progress and effectiveness of your program.

An important point regarding metrics is to begin with some basic metrics and modify them over time. You will never know if your program is improving unless you are measuring it, and you should start immediately rather than waiting to develop more complicated metrics.

Change Management

It takes a considerable amount of time to harden a server or configure a firewall to ensure that adequate security controls are in place. If a well-meaning staff member makes a temporary change to a firewall to allow broader access for a period but forgets to remove this access, you become exposed. When taken in a broader context, a medium-sized company might have hundreds of servers, multiple firewalls, and so on that are constantly undergoing some amount of change, and this has to be controlled.

Change management ensures that these modifications to your environment occur in a controlled manner. This includes having formal processes to ensure that changes to critical components of your infrastructure are documented, approved, and implemented in a controlled manner.

Solutions in this area are quite simple and require a formal documented process to ensure that necessary controls are in place, along with periodic testing to ensure that your staff follows them. Whenever possible, you should also turn on any audit and logging capabilities in your environment to ensure that you can track who has made these changes and periodically review these logs to ensure that they are appropriate.

Future Technology Architecture

Referencing the industry best practices that you learned in this chapter, you can use the information security evaluation framework to design your future technology architecture. It is important to identify those areas that you must address first; you will use this information later when you develop your information security roadmap.

Use the scorecard in Table 6-4 to summarize the future technology architecture for your company. Identify the areas of highest importance and focus your resources in the areas that will provide the best protection to your company. Use a "0" to indicate that this area is not important for your company, "1" for partial implementation, and "2" for full implementation.

Table 6-4

Information Security Future Technology Architecture

Component	Current Score (0–2)	Desired Future Score (0–2)	Priority (High, Medium, Low)	Desired Time Frame	Comments
Strategy					
■ Comprehensive information security architecture					
■ Computing environment segmented into security zones					
■ Security layered at gateway, server, and client					
■ Security roadmap includes both strategic and tactical objectives					
■ Strategy supports current models for conducting business					
Components					
■ AAA					
■ Anti-virus					
■ Firewalls					
■ Vulnerability management					
■ Intrusion detection					
Administration					
■ Regular scanning and remediation program					
■ Quarterly penetration testing					
■ Annual independent audit of security program					
■ Regular update of anti-virus definitions					
■ Change management					
■ Reporting on security incidents and initiatives to executive management and board of directors					
Total Score (0–32)					

Technology Summary

Technology is the final component of your program, and it must be carefully architected and deployed for your program to be effective. Your security architecture must be tightly aligned with your business model to ensure that you are protecting the critical assets of the organization. Technology can be expensive to implement, and you cannot afford to waste this precious resource on areas that are not vital to the long-term success of the organization.

Armed with this information for the third component of your program, you are now ready to design the roadmap for your future information security program. It's important to strike a balance between the people, process, and technology components of your program. We will discuss this process in the next chapter.

Key Points for This Chapter

- Technology can be used to enforce your information security processes and is an essential component of an effective program.

- A comprehensive information security architecture is necessary to ensure that your program supports your current and future business model.

- Defense-in-depth can be used to develop multiple layers of protection within your organization and offer higher levels of protection for your most valuable assets.

- Authentication, authorization, and accounting (AAA), firewalls, and anti-virus software are the most basic security technologies; they are required for almost every organization.

- Information security is dynamic, and regular scanning of your environment for vulnerabilities is necessary to identify areas for remediation.

- Security metrics are important to measure the effectiveness of your program and monitor progress over time.
- Independent review of your security program is recommended to ensure that your staff has not overlooked potential areas of vulnerability.

Chapter 7

Information Security Roadmap

A former employee of a major Internet provider was charged with stealing the company's entire subscriber list of more than 30 million consumers and their 90 million screen names. The former employee copied the company's subscriber list in May of 2003 and then sold this information to another individual, who used this list to promote his Internet gambling business. This individual then resold the list again for $52,000 to another spammer, who used the email addresses to market herbal penile enlargement pills.

Access to the company's 30 million consumer records was restricted; however, the former employee impersonated another employee to gain access to this information. He was able to steal zips codes, credit card types, and telephone numbers in addition to screen names and email addresses. A search of his computer revealed an electronic conversation between the thieves describing the heist and numerous attempts to find the subscription names stored across multiple computers. Both of these individuals face up to five years in prison; however, the impact on the company's brand will last much longer.

These individuals collaborated closely to access critical customer information and use it for personal gain. Your organization needs to work to develop your information security roadmap to defend your company against current and future threats like these.

Introduction

You can use an information security roadmap to help lead your information security program, consolidate all the information you've accumulated thus far, choose alternatives for remediation and funding, and establish priorities for your implementation plan. Finally, you can divide the plan into projects and begin securing your information systems.

Heightened awareness of information security issues will contribute to your organization's ability to evaluate its security needs and develop an effective security strategy to guide it toward implementing a revised and improved program in the future.

Heightened awareness of security will also help your company identify and address tactical issues that require immediate attention and remediation. Awareness can lead to renewed commitment from key members of the management team, without whom you would have a much more difficult time securing resources for your program.

Overview

The third and final step of the *information security architecture methodology* concentrates on developing your information security roadmap to the future. The first step you completed included analyzing your overall business requirements and serves as the framework for your program. During the second step, you evaluated the three components of your current architecture (people, process, and technology) and defined your desired future architecture. In the final step, you will use this information to evaluate alternative methods of achieving the goals for your future program.

You will continue your evaluation based upon the people, process, and technology components of your program. You need to balance these essential building blocks carefully to ensure the long-term success of your program.

You must train your *people* and hold them accountable for running your information security program. You must develop *processes* to ensure that all members of your organization understand their role in protecting your company. Finally, you must use *technology* to ensure that your security staff has the tools necessary to support your program.

High-Level Information Security Concepts

When developing your information security program, some important concepts to drive your processes are *confidentiality, integrity, and availability* (CIA), *least privilege,* and *speed versus control.* These concepts span the people, process, and technology components of your program. You should consider these principles both when developing your strategy and during routine management.

CIA is an important concept that you need to consider, especially when establishing your overall strategy. *Confidentiality* ensures that your program protects sensitive information from unauthorized access or disclosure. Confidentiality includes the use of transmission encryption (such as the use of SSL on web sites to enter personally identifiable information) and the use of storage encryption (for encrypting personally identifiable information stored in customer information databases). You must implement access controls to ensure that only authorized personnel are able to access information and that unauthorized personnel cannot recover deleted information.

Integrity ensures that unauthorized persons cannot alter or delete information. The last thing you would want is for an unauthorized person to alter your company's vital documents, such as financial records.

Availability means that information will be accessible by authorized individuals when, where, and how they need it. It doesn't make sense to have all these controls in place if authorized personnel can't get to the information they need to perform their jobs.

Least privilege requires that you provide employees with access to the information that they require to perform their jobs and no more. For example, although all employees might have access to the company's expense reimbursement system, only your manager can approve your expense report. Your manager's access is restricted to approving his employee's expense reports, but not his own expense report or those belonging to another organization's employees. Thus, employees can perform their jobs without additional systems access. You should consider applying *least privilege* throughout your program because extending access beyond what someone requires when performing his job can increase your organization's risk.

Another critical component of your overall strategy is balancing the *speed and control* elements of your program. Figure 7-1 provides a graphic representation of this balancing act.

Information Security Balancing Act

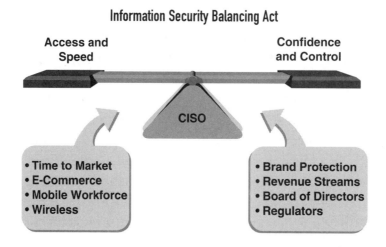

Figure 7-1   Information security program balancing act.

All businesses are under tremendous pressure to offer new products and services. For the toy industry, the ability to ship a new product in advance of a key date, such as the start of the Christmas shopping season, can determine the success or failure of the company. Many companies rely heavily on the Internet, and their customers expect access to this delivery channel at all times.

You must evaluate these types of pressure against the risks of security incidents, which can affect your company's brand and revenue streams. Your customers rely on you to have access controls in place that will protect their sensitive personal information, such as credit card numbers. Some industries, including financial services or health care, must demonstrate that required controls are in place just to continue operations.

It's easy to err on the conservative side and demand that your company makes security issues the highest priority; however, this doesn't necessarily make sense from an overall business perspective.

Your information security program needs to have the appropriate processes in place to enable your staff to assess risks and make sound decisions for balancing program priorities. Risk analysis and management need to be included in the process for determining which products and services you will offer. Waiting until just before launch time will increase both the risk and remediation costs. It is important to keep these high-level concepts in mind when developing your program and making critical decisions.

Information Security Assessment Summary

The vital statistics of your information security program include the people, processes, and technology components of your program. By closely evaluating these areas, you will have a good idea of your current state and can begin to develop your improvement plan.

You can use the *information security evaluation framework* described in Chapter 3 to determine how effective your existing information security program is. You used this framework in Chapters 4, "People," 5, "Process," and 6, "Technology," to evaluate the people, processes, and technology components of your program. This framework is based upon 50 of the most important industry best practices for information security, and you can grade these elements of your program to determine an overall score of 0–100. You can summarize the result of your baseline assessment into an overall scorecard for your program, which you can use to identify potential areas for improvement. You can then use this information, along with your organization's level of investment, to develop your information security roadmap. Table 7-1 provides an example of a completed security assessment.

Table 7-1

Information Security Existing Program Evaluation Summary		
Program Component	**Score**	**Comments**
People		
■ Strategy	7	■ No formal strategy exists today
■ Components	8	■ Staff focused on day-to-day firefighting
■ Administration	9	■ Minimal involvement of executive staff
People Score	**24**	
Process		
■ Strategy	10	■ Informal policies that are not followed consistently
■ Components	9	■ Policies are not easily accessed by employees
■ Administration	7	■ All major security policies have been considered in program
Process Score	**26**	
Technology		
■ Strategy	6	■ No technology architecture in place, and changes are tactical in nature
■ Components	10	■ Major technology components have been deployed
■ Administration	10	■ Informal program to protect environments from security threats
Technology Score	**26**	
Overall Average Rating (0–100)	**76**	

In Table 7-1, the company's program has achieved an overall score of 76 out of 100. The scorecard identifies the areas with the lowest scores, which should be the first areas to address.

By taking this analysis a step further, you can determine how well your company is doing compared to similar companies in your industry. A small mining company with few automated processes will require a different information security program from a financial services company that conducts the majority of its business electronically.

You can use the *information security business dependency matrix* from Chapter 3 for this purpose. This matrix takes into account the unique characteristics of your company and the industry you are serving to determine your dependency on information security. Table 7-2 provides an example of a completed matrix.

Table 7-2

Information Security Business Dependency Matrix	
Component	**Ratings (High–3, Medium–2, Low–1)**
Company Characteristics	
Dependence upon systems to offer products and services to customers	2
Value of company's intellectual property stored in electronic form	2
Requirement for 24-7 business systems	3
Degree of change within company (expansions, M&A, new markets)	1
Business size (number of offices, number of customers, level of revenue) and complexity (processes, systems, products)	1
Industry Characteristics	
Budget for security administration and security initiatives	1
Potential impact to national or critical infrastructure	1
Customer sensitivity to security and privacy	3
Level of industry regulation regarding security (GLBA, HIPAA)	1
Brand or revenue impact of security incident	3
Extent of business operations dependent upon third parties (partners, suppliers)	2
Customers' ability to quickly switch vendors based upon vendors' ability to offer services in a secure manner	3
Average Overall Ranking (Total Scores/12)	2

In this example, the company has a medium overall ranking for business dependency upon information security. This is a smaller company that is not experiencing a lot of change and that has not traditionally devoted a large portion of its budget to information security. It does require its systems to be operational on a 24-7 basis, though, and its customers are sensitive to security incidents and can easily switch to a competitor.

By combining the overall rating of your program with your company's dependency upon information security, you can develop an overall assessment of your program. These two factors will enable you to answer the critical question of how well your existing information security program is performing. It might not be necessary to make major investments in your program if the security risks are low for your company. Table 7-3 provides some guidelines for combining this information to develop an overall assessment.

Table 7-3

Information Security Program Assessment Scoring

Business Dependency	Program Rating	Overall Assessment
High	95–100	Good
	90–94	Average
	Below 90	Poor
Medium	90–100	Good
	80–89	Average
	Below 80	Poor
Low	85–100	Good
	70–84	Average
	Below 70	Poor

In our previous example, the company had a medium dependency on information security and an overall program rating of 76. Using the program assessment in Table 7-3, you would rate this program *poor*.

You can use this matrix as a general guideline for evaluating your information security program. At this point, you are in a position to use the information gathered in this analysis to begin the process of identifying alternatives to reach your desired future state for your program. Next, you will move on to the *information security gap analysis* process, which you can use to identify alternatives and develop suggestions for choosing the appropriate plan for your company.

Information Security Gap Analysis

At this point, you should have a good understanding of how your existing information security program is operating along with how well it compares to similar companies in your industry. The next step in the process includes identifying alternatives to move from your current to your future information security program. This section provides some guidelines on how to develop those alternatives and a rational approach for evaluation.

Completing the first two steps of the *information security architecture methodology* should have provided you with the following information:

- **Current state of your information security program**—Includes what is working, and what needs to be improved

- **Business requirements analysis**—Includes guiding principles for your information security program and your company's dependence upon information security

- **Desired future state of your information security program**—Includes specific recommendations for people, process, and technology components of the program

This provides you with the information you need to develop your information security gap analysis. This analysis should separate your activities into those that are strategic and essential to the long-term success of your program and those tactical items that you need to address as soon as possible. You should also prioritize these gaps into high, medium, and low so that you can understand the relative importance of each area.

If one of your company's strategic objectives is increasing customer's trust when using your online commerce system, but you have made only minimal investments in information security, you would have a large gap to meet these objectives. On the other hand, informal processes in place at a small company might be a minor gap because the organization has not grown to the size where a more formal program of processes is necessary.

By using the evaluation of the *people, process,* and *technology* components of your information security program that you developed in Chapters 4, 5, and 6, you can identify gaps between your current and desired architecture.

A high gap indicates that a significant amount of work will be required to transform a component of your existing program into its desired future state. If the desired state is to have a responsive information security organization, but the current staff spends the majority of its time in *firefighting* tactical mode, you should consider this a high gap.

Table 7-4 provides a high-level example of gap analysis that you can modify for use at your company.

Table 7-4

Information Security Gap Analysis

Component	Current Score	Desired Future Score	Priority (High, Medium, Low)	Desired Time Frame	Comments
People					
■ Strategy	7	12	High	12 months	■ No formal strategy exists today
■ Components	8	10	Medium	18 months	■ Staff focused on day-to-day fire-fighting
■ Administration	9	10	Low	24 months	■ Minimal involvement of executive staff
People Summary	24	32			
Process					
■ Strategy	10	12	High	12 months	■ Informal policies that are not followed consistently
■ Components	9	10	Low	24 months	■ Policies are not easily accessed by employees
■ Administration	7	8	Low	18 months	■ All major security policies have been considered in program
Process Summary	26	30			

continues

Component	Current Score	Desired Future Score	Priority (High, Medium, Low)	Desired Time Frame	Comments
Technology					
■ Strategy	6	8	Medium	12 months	■ No technology architecture in place, andchanges are tactical in nature
■ Components	10	10	Low	24 months	■ Major technology components have been deployed
■ Administration	10	10	Low	24 months	■ Informal program to protect environments from security threats
Technology Summary	26	28			
Total Score (0–100)	76	90			

In this example, several components of the existing information security program score far below the desired future state. This provides a starting point to evaluate alternatives to bridge these gaps. It's important to conduct the initial gap analysis without regard to the time or cost to bridge the gap; that comes later. The natural tendency at this point is to start thinking about solutions for your company. When the company begins to understand the nature of these gaps, you are in a position to evaluate the time and investment necessary to achieve the desired future state.

Options to Bridge Information Security Gaps

Information security is no different from the other investments that your company needs to consider when allocating resources. From an overall funding perspective, no absolute guidelines exist for information security spending. A company with a greater emphasis on security, such as a financial services firm, will invest more in security than most manufacturers or retailers. Industry averages range from 2% to 10% or more of the information technology budget being dedicated to information security.

Armed with the results of your gap analysis, you can produce your information security roadmap and use it to provide management with multiple alternatives for bridging these gaps. One alternative is to use the time dimension of your roadmap to offer funding choices. If your program must be in place quickly, you're more likely to incur additional expenses than if your roadmap extends the implementation of the project over the course of a year. Other areas to consider include the following:

- Information security is similar to insurance, and the benefits are often weighed against the probability of something happening to your company.

- Use the return on investment approach to balance the cost of a security initiative with the expected benefits.

- Estimate the costs of system downtime over various periods.

- Include both initial and ongoing costs of the security program.

The results of this analysis enable your company to determine the appropriate level of investment in your information security program. Table 7-5 provides an example of strategic alternatives that you can use for your company.

Table 7-5

Information Security Strategic Alternatives

Alternative		Time Frame	Estimated Costs	Benefits
Aggressive implementation	■ Hire third-party integrator to accelerate information security implementation ■ Create CISO position and hire experienced leader ■ Establish corporate governance board to oversee program	6–12 months	$5–10 million	■ Continue e-commerce initiative ■ $4 million revenue opportunity
Accelerated implementation	■ Hire third party to assist in information security program implementation ■ Create separate information security organization and hire experienced leader ■ Provide management team with regular updates on program	12–18 months	$3–5 million	■ Delay e-commerce initiative ■ $2 million revenue opportunity
Incremental improvements	■ Leverage third parties in selected areas ■ Establish training program for information security staff ■ Formalize program and provide regular updates on progress	18–24 Months	$1–2 million	■ Postpone e-commerce initiative ■ No revenue opportunity

The list of strategic alternatives for your company might be different; however, the tradeoff between the level of investment and the expected time to complete this work will be similar. Carefully evaluate these alternatives against other strategic initiatives that are competing for your company's finite internal resources. You should view security as an ongoing capital investment because short-term investments do not ensure the long-term success of your program.

Information Security Roadmap

After you have determined the appropriate level of investment for your company, you can convert your selected strategic alternative into an *information security roadmap*.

Your roadmap should include the strategic initiatives that you expect to accomplish over the next couple of years in addition to plans to address any tactical issues.

You should closely monitor progress against your roadmap because your program will probably represent a major investment for your company, and you will want to ensure continued support from your management team. Table 7-6 provides an example of an information security roadmap.

Table 7-6

Information Security Roadmap				
Component	**Strategic Initiatives**	**Time Frame**	**Tactical Plans**	**Time Frame**
People	■ Develop information security strategy	6 months	■ Assign acting manager for department	30 days
	■ Create and staff separate information security organization	12 months	■ Clarify roles and responsibilities for information security	60 days
	■ Establish formal training program to receive industry-recognized credentials	24 months	■ Schedule firewall training for all staff	90 days

continues

Component	Strategic Initiatives	Time Frame	Tactical Plans	Time Frame
Processes	■ Establish corporate governance board with key members of management team	9 months	■ Collect existing security policies	30 days
	■ Publish security policies on company intranet	9 months	■ Develop consistent format for policies	90 days
	■ Establish company-wide security awareness program	18 months	■ Engage with legal and HR on existing policies	90 days
Technology	■ Establish technology architecture	12 months	■ Scan environment and remedy high vulnerabilities	90 days
	■ Provide regular reporting on effectiveness of program	18 months	■ Update virus definitions for all employees	30 days
	■ Have independent third-party audit program	12 months	■ Document changes to computing infrastructure	90 days

This roadmap summarizes both the strategic and tactical objectives of the program for the next two years. Tactical issues will continue to occur; however, it's important to focus on the strategic initiatives. Due to the dynamic nature of information security, you will need to revise your plan over the course of the year. Plan for a major annual reevaluation and revision and reevaluate your investment level during your regular budgeting cycles.

In this case, your information security program is divided into a six-section matrix, looking at the people, process, and technology components of your program. The remediation processes required for these components is divided into strategic and tactical initiatives. Strategic initiatives are defined as requiring efforts from multiple business units or taking up to a year to accomplish, and tactical initiatives are defined as efforts that require input from a single business unit or that take three months or less for remediation. You can compare priorities from each section of the matrix to formulate a master priority list.

Sticking to the simple remediation efforts in the beginning can yield tremendous results. This is relatively easy, and it creates organization-wide awareness of the problems, secures the targets that are most tempting to malicious individuals, and enables your staff to build a sense of purpose and accomplishment for themselves and the rest of the organization.

Ensuring that your business is no longer susceptible to the vulnerabilities listed on the SANS (SysAdmin, Audit, Network, Security, Institute) Top Twenty vulnerabilities list eliminates an enormous number of risks in your environment. Vendor-supplied patches are available for all 20 of the vulnerabilities listed, so there is absolutely no excuse for these vulnerabilities to persist in your environment. They are all well-known and relatively easy to address.

You need to balance the addressing of tactical concerns against achieving the overall goals of the program because you need to migrate from *firefighting* mode to *fire prevention*. This isn't a simple task, and the leader of the information security program will have to make these decisions on a regular basis. Your information security program's development will be a constant journey, not a destination.

The next step is to expand your information security roadmap into an implementation plan. This requires the development of detailed project plans to accomplish the broad strategies that you have established. Figure 7-2 provides a template you can use to capture this information and provide management reporting on progress.

Information Security Project Template

Project: E-Commerce Site Security	Project Review Dates Last: July 1, 2004 This: Aug 1, 2004 Next: Sept 1, 2004

Strategy: Address short-term issues with securing the e-commerce site	IT Project Owner: Applicaions Director
	Customer/Department: Sales and Marketing

Results Last 30 Days
- Updated the security patches for hardware supporting the e-commerce site
- Established regular monitoring program to manually monitor site and ensure it is functioning properly

Plans Next 30 Days
- Evaluate automated monitoring tools
- Complete interview process and hire additional security staff

Items for Attention
- Major software upgrade required in future

Project Milestones	Data	Status	Budget	Amount
Patch hardware and software	July 1	100%	• Consulting	$100K
Manual monitoring process	July 1	100%	• Hardware	$200K
Hire additional security staff	Aug 1	50%	• Software	$150K
Automate monitoring process	Aug 1	50%		
Upgrade to new e-commerce software	Sept 1	25%		
Train marketing staff on new processes	Sept 1	25%		

Figure 7-2   Information security project template.

At a minimum, you should expand your information security roadmap into six projects that correspond to the six-section matrix of your roadmap. This enables you to keep track of both strategic and tactical plans for the people, process, and technology components of your program. Larger organizations can have many more projects depending upon the size and complexity of their business operations.

Information Security Roadmap Summary

The reality of building a comprehensive information security program is that you need to employ skilled people, implement processes that all people can adapt to their organizations, and back it up with effective technology. Everything must work together; without one of these pieces, you will not have a sufficient security program in place. One weak link in the information security triangle, and your program collapses. Whether you are the CEO, COO, or CIO, you represent the quality of your enterprise's security practice, and ultimately you will be responsible if there is a breach. Don't take that chance!

Key Points for This Chapter

- Your information security roadmap can be used to guide your program to your future desired state.

- Confidentiality, integrity, and availability (CIA) are fundamental concepts for any effective information security program.

- Information security is a balancing act between speed of offering new products and services and confidence that those products and services will be delivered in a secure manner.

- The security evaluation framework can be used to develop strategic alternatives for your program and establish a roadmap that is appropriate for your company.

- Tactical initiatives must be carefully evaluated to ensure that the overall strategic components of your program are being addressed.

- Security project templates can be an effective method for tracking the progress of your program in a consistent manner.

Chapter 8

View Into the Future

A major U.S. bank has been the target of repeated phishing schemes that attempt to defraud the bank's retail customers. Phishing is the use of fraudulent email to lure someone into divulging private information to a bogus web site or email address. These attacks have included a message threatening to close the customer's account if the customer does not disclose personal information, messages from the business's "security department" seeking account information to help the company upgrade its computer servers, and its "accounts department" seeking credit card information so that customers can "maintain the company experience."

This has been a nightmare for the company because it must try to maintain the confidence of its customers and repair the damage to its brand. The latest email scam indicates to unsuspecting customers that accounts connected with money laundering, credit card fraud, terrorism, and credit fraud activity have been blocked and encourages the customers to check their account balances. The email also provides a link to a bogus web site that lures unsuspecting customers into disclosing personal information.

As we have described throughout this book, the increased amount of business conducted electronically has attracted criminals to the Internet. The demographics of attacks will shift from gaining public notoriety to financial gain and, as we will see in this chapter, increasingly includes elements of organized crime. This chapter provides some insight into the future and how to protect your company from falling victim to these attacks.

Introduction

The future of information security offers some scenarios that have the potential to affect your industry and business; however, it is not entirely clear exactly what will happen. These scenarios might require that your company spend more time and money on your information security program to ensure that you are successful, particularly for companies that conduct a portion of their business electronically.

By understanding the possibilities, you will be in a better position to address them in the future. Ignoring these issues or assuming they will not affect your business is not going to position you to provide the best service possible to your customers and stay ahead of the competition.

Overview

This chapter covers two broad topics: the evolution of information security threats and industry solutions that address these threats. The information security field is changing rapidly, and this will continue for quite some time. Internet use continues to grow, and as we have mentioned previously, because the Internet was designed as an open system to facilitate the exchange of information, security is not its main strength.

Some of the major threats to information systems and what your company can do to prepare for these threats are discussed herein. We also review industry solutions to provide some insight into the challenges that you must face to improve commercially available products.

Threat Evolution

You can expect future threats to be even more serious and challenging than those that your organization currently faces. This evolution includes more complex threats, faster spreading threats, and a shift in hacker intentions and demographics.

This trend requires businesses, governments, and academic organizations to adapt to the future electronic battlefield. The amount of business you conduct electronically, including transactions over the Internet, will continue to grow, so you must put an information security program in place to ensure that your business is protected.

More Complex Threats

Information security threats have evolved from the minor annoyance of a simple computer virus to major disruptions of global enterprises from blended threats. Although a virus might have caused an individual worker to lose files and perhaps a few hours of productivity, blended threats such as Nimda and Code Red actually shut down major corporations for multiple days.

Corporations currently measure the damage from these incidents in billions of dollars. Future threats have the possibility of causing global damage by disrupting the availability of the Internet or attacking infrastructure including water, power, and communications. The possible damage isn't only financial; it can also include the loss of human lives. Figure 8-1 provides a graphic overview of this evolution.

Information Security Threat Evolution

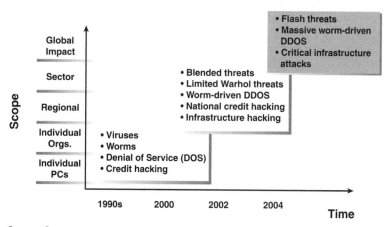

Source: Symantec

Figure 8-1   General security threat evolution.

Like early threats such as viruses, *Denial of Service* (DoS) attacks targeted individual computers and caused disruption. Even these relatively unsophisticated attacks garnered the attention of the media and of corporate executives. During this time, simple attacks such as defacing web sites were considered newsworthy. However, today web site defacements are so common that the media no longer tracks or reports them. Over time, threats have become more complex, and their impact scope has expanded. Writers' abilities have evolved to the point where they can create *worms,* which are much more destructive and which no longer require human intervention to spread. Originally, to infect a computer, a simple virus required the victim to take an action such as opening an email attachment or an infected file. Today, worms can spread unaided after they have copied themselves onto an unprotected host.

DoS attacks have evolved into *Distributed Denial of Service Attacks* (DDoS) that use many computers to launch an attack instead of a single system. This makes it difficult to prevent the attack or identify the actual attacker. The economic impact of these threats has also increased, with other crimes such as credit card fraud now involving millions of stolen credit card numbers, often with the involvement of organized crime.

Recent attacks have increased in scope, and targets now include critical infrastructures. For two weeks in 2001, hackers attacked the California Independent System Operator and came close to disrupting electrical transmission across the state. A hacker in Australia, in 2000, succeeded in causing a sewage treatment system to leak hundreds of thousands of gallons of raw sewage into Queensland parks, rivers, and even the Hyatt Regency Hotel. These attacks targeted critical infrastructures and had more far-reaching impacts than attacks against individuals or corporations.

In the future, your business will face threats that are even more complex. As we have mentioned, *blended threats* use multiple attack vectors to replicate and cause damage; the Nimda Worm used five different vectors to infect companies. Professionals knew about all these vulnerabilities in advance; however, this was the first time that a worm used them in combination.

We can predict with high confidence that future threats will utilize larger combinations of vulnerabilities. There are literally thousands of known vulnerabilities today, and someone will eventually assemble a combination of threats that will circumvent available tools used to prevent worms from spreading. Addressing future threats will require information security organizations to revise their security programs to minimize damage.

Beyond blended threats, a possible future step in threat evolution is *flash threats,* complex threats with great speed that will move across the Internet in seconds. Your company will not have adequate time to react to these threats; therefore, it will need to rethink its security strategy before these attacks happen. Another possibility is massive worm-driven DDOS attacks that disrupt services across the world. These attacks can target individual nations' infrastructures and disrupt basic services including electricity. In general, as threats evolve from targeted hacking to flash threats, expect to see a shift from localized short-term disruption to major global disruptions.

Faster Spreading Threats

All future threats will spread much more quickly than older ones. Early viruses took weeks or even months to spread, whereas Code Red infected more than 350,000 hosts in just 14 hours, and Slammer infected most vulnerable hosts in just 10 minutes. As advances in technology accelerate the rate of communication, they will also speed up the spread of threats. Figure 8-2 provides an overview of the emergence of new types of malicious code over time.

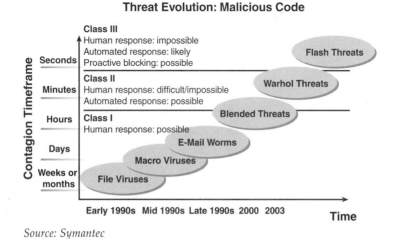

Source: *Symantec*

Figure 8-2   Threat evolution: malicious code.

One way of categorizing these threats is to place them into classes according to the amount of time required for a majority of vulnerable hosts to become infected. (This isn't a formal categorization used by the information security industry.) For illustrative purposes, they are called *Class I, Class II,* and *Class III* threats. Class I threats can take days or even weeks to spread, Class II threats spread in hours or even minutes, and Class III threats will require only seconds. Responses to these threats have evolved from effective human response in the past to reliance upon automation and proactive technology in the future.

Class I Threats

To date, most attacks have fallen into Class I threats, taking days or hours to spread. Initially, viruses required months to spread because they required human interaction, such as opening an infected email attachment that contains the virus. Response to these threats included updating virus definitions, and infections were often isolated to a small portion of employees at a company. These threats evolved to more advanced email worms, such as the *Melissa Virus* that didn't require human action and could spread in days.

Blended threats such as Nimda and Code Red reduced the infection time to hours and started to reach the upper limits of human response. Responses to blended threats included updating virus definitions and applying software patches to vulnerable computers. The increased contagion rate and amount of work required for remediation placed additional pressure on addressing these threats in a timely manner, increasing the impact of these threats.

Class II Threats

Class II threats will spread across the Internet in a matter of a few hours to minutes. In 2002, Nicholas Weaver, a graduate student at U.C. Berkeley, published "Warhol Worms: The Potential for Very Fast Internet Plagues," a paper predicting that a computer worm could theoretically bring down the entire Internet in 15 minutes.

He named his theoretical worm after Andy Warhol, referencing Warhol's famous quote, "In the future, everyone will be famous for fifteen minutes."

It is hard to prove his theory; however, it does raise the question of the potential impact of the Internet being down for a period of time, a so-called Internet snow day. Imagine the number of organizations that rely upon the Internet and how difficult it would be to continue operations without this resource.

The Slammer Worm was the first attack to incorporate the concepts outlined in the "Warhol Worms" paper. Slammer spread quickly, with its infection rate doubling every 8.5 seconds in the initial stages. It was able to infect 90% of vulnerable hosts in just 10 minutes. Slammer infected approximately 75,000 hosts, caused 13,000 bank ATM machines to be unavailable, and even prompted the cancellation of some airline flights. We can expect future attacks to follow similar patterns of rapid deployment across the Internet. Human response becomes difficult or impossible for addressing such threats, although an automated response would be possible within these timeframes.

Class III Threats

Class III threats will spread across the Internet in a matter of minutes to seconds. Flash threats are examples of Class III threats discussed in current research literature. These threats could identify and spread to a large percentage of susceptible targets within seconds. We haven't seen any true Flash threats, but they are likely to occur in the not-so-distant future.

The initial outbreak of Flash threats will require proactive technologies for defense because the time required to react is much too short for a human or an automated response. Organizations will use proactive technologies to provide protection while automated responses determine the nature of the threat and respond accordingly.

Zero-Day Attacks

Hackers exploit vulnerabilities—including defects in software—to perform an unauthorized activity. Typically, this occurs sometime after experts have identified the vulnerability. The industry refers to the time between discovering a vulnerability and the release of a threat to exploit it as the *vulnerability-threat window*.

High-profile attacks such as Nimda and Slammer all had vulnerability-threat windows of many months, leaving plenty of time for the vendor to create a patch and the public to be warned, reducing potential threat damage. Thus far, the shortest period for a vulnerability to be exploited after a patch was available was 2 days for the Witty Worm.

On the average, exploits have appeared six months after public disclosure of a vulnerability. Figure 8-3 provides a graphic overview of these timeframes.

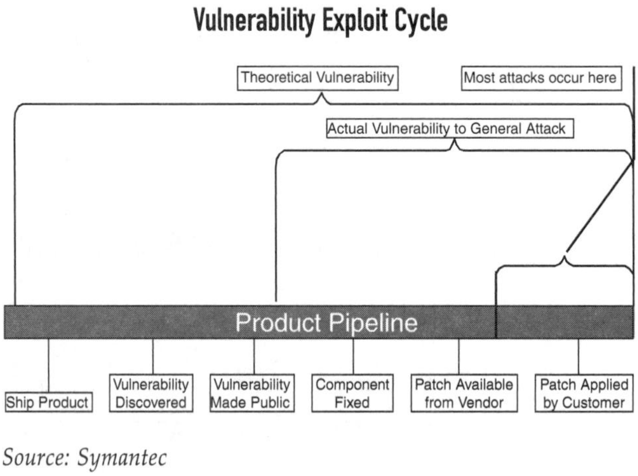

Vulnerability Exploit Cycle

Source: Symantec

Figure 8-3 Vulnerability—exploit cycle.

In a future *zero-day* scenario, hackers will create and release an exploit with no advance notice that the vulnerability exists. A *zero-day* threat poses a considerable problem for organizations. Because remedies to address the vulnerability aren't yet available, an organization cannot take preventative measures to mitigate this risk. Compare this scenario to the outbreak of a human virus previously unknown to doctors—the result would be widespread infection and deaths.

Companies will have to react much more quickly before these threats can disrupt their business operations. They need to monitor their own systems to detect any potential threats and have crisp response procedures in place. This includes tuning the people, process, and technology components of your program to deal with these threats quickly because an hour might be too late in the future.

Shift in Hacker Demographics and Intentions

Cyberspace will become one of the battlefields of the future. Countries with significant military resources will find themselves having to address new threats from entities that they might not have considered threats in the past. Increasing dependence upon computer systems for communications, commerce, and management of basic infrastructure underscores this point.

Amateurs, often teenagers, release many of the most damaging threats with no particular target in mind. The Nimda and Klez worms didn't target a specific organization, but they still did an enormous amount of damage.

However, as governments and businesses move additional critical functions online, you should expect to see a shift in attacker demographics, from the amateur hacker to better-funded and more dedicated attackers who are are affiliated with organized crime, terrorist organizations, and rogue nations. These attackers will have more specific targets and motivations.

You can expect to see a reduction in the vulnerability-threat window as this shift occurs. Searching for vulnerabilities and quickly creating exploits is likely to be a time-consuming and expensive task, requiring the efforts of more heavily funded attackers. Figure 8-4 provides some insight into this shift in hacker demographics.

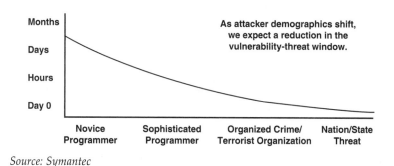

Figure 8-4   Hacker demographics shift.

Critical infrastructure such as power, water, transportation, and communications systems rely heavily upon computer systems. Past efforts to prevent physical and logical attacks to these resources have been effective; however, the future will require organizations and governments to put more elaborate information security programs in place.

An individual or group with limited resources might be able to disrupt critical systems in the future, operating from a country that does not have the time or resources to address these issues. *Cyber terrorism* will not require extensive resources because many tools used by hackers are available on the Internet for free.

As the military increasingly relies on computer systems for communications and weapons, information security plays a more important role in their operations. The risk of an enemy intercepting key communications has severe consequences and can cost many lives. Heavier reliance upon computer-based weapons requires that an effective security program be in place to ensure that these systems are secure. This responsibility extends to industry partners developing weapon systems for the military because a breach in their environment might result in the loss of plans or source code. An enemy who has limited resources could shift the balance of power if he were able to break into these weapon systems and disrupt their operations.

Credit, debit, and *smart cards* supporting millions of transactions per day are rapidly replacing cash and checks. The ability to offer products and services electronically is an accepted and expected method of conducting business. Criminals always follow the money, and this is too large of an opportunity to escape their notice.

Law enforcement agencies need to understand these challenges and adapt their programs accordingly. This will require a shift from the more traditional methods of law enforcement to electronic methods of crime prevention. Electronic forensics have become increasingly more important because electronic evidence is required to convict many felons. Corporations will also need to incorporate these challenges into their plans to ensure that they are not exposed. This will require an increased level of communication between corporate and government organizations in the future.

Solution Evolution Trends

Major trends for the information security industry include simplification, proactive security, and improved management. Many of the solutions offered by information security vendors are too complex, and it can be difficult to deploy and manage the solutions required to protect your business. Also, most security products operate in reactive mode and will not address the increased speed and complexity of future threats. This is due in part to the immaturity of the market; eventually, the industry will grow to offer solutions that address these challenges.

Simplification

The large numbers of *point solutions* that exist to solve each security problem are evidence of the immaturity of the information security market. As more threats appear, the industry creates individual products that address specific threats. We are now at a stage when the number and complexity of information security products is beginning to create problems. This phenomenon will need to change in the future.

This is similar to other industries prior to the emergence of leaders that established standard solutions. *Enterprise resource planning* (ERP) vendors revolutionized the enterprise software industry and now offer complete solutions to run your business operations. Eventually, a small number of vendors will emerge as the leaders of the information security industry and establish standards for the rest of the industry. Either these leaders will acquire smaller vendors, or these smaller companies will have to integrate their products with the leaders' to be successful.

Many security products also require a server to host the application. Each additional security product can increase your infrastructure costs because you have to buy hardware, operating system software, and so on, and your staff must harden and maintain the new server. The emergence of security appliances, which strive to integrate multiple independent hardware and software components, is another step toward simplification of the industry.

One solution is to put multiple security products such as firewalls and anti-virus software on an appliance running an operating system such as Linux, for which there are relatively few viruses or exploits. You can deploy multiple security products delivered on an appliance that the vendor has already hardened. The information security staff can configure these devices centrally and ship them to remote staff who can complete the installation process. The staff can then perform management and ongoing support remotely, which reduces ongoing maintenance costs.

Over time, vendors will embed information security products in other devices, and your staff will use them as standalone solutions less often. This requires a major shift by enterprise software vendors to address security as a key feature in their products, as opposed to the current approach of bolting on security later. This shift toward a much simpler and more integrated information security approach will greatly improve protection for your organization.

Proactive Security

One of the major shortcomings of current information security products is that they don't proactively protect your computing environment. Vulnerability management tools can take a snapshot of your environment and identify potential vulnerabilities, but a snapshot is not *real-time,* and your business changes on a daily basis. You can fix issues that you identify; however, if another exploit or vulnerability appears tomorrow, you will have to repeat the process. Intrusion detection tools operate after the fact by alerting you of attacks that have taken place in your environment. This is helpful; however, IDS does little to actually stop the attack from taking place.

A more effective system is necessary, one that integrates the reactive capabilities of intrusion detection with the proactive ability of vulnerability management and that can address issues in real-time. The goal is to have an intrusion detection tool that identifies the problem and alerts you but that also goes one step further by taking an action to protect your systems.

Ideally, such a tool would immediately do something about an intrusion, such as change the configuration on a firewall to block an attack. This removes the delay associated with having your staff try to address the problem because human beings cannot react quickly enough. The industry refers to this type of software as an *intrusion prevention tool* because it combines the proactive and reactive capabilities of other security products.

Improved Information Security Management

The sheer amount of data that current information security devices generate is overwhelming. Each information security product generates its own version of logs, events, and alerts that your staff must evaluate to determine which responses are appropriate. Due to the absence of widely adopted industry standards, products don't create this information in a consistent fashion, and your security personnel must correlate this data before they can use it.

In the past, businesses faced this same challenge when dealing with high volumes of financial and operations data. In response, they developed decision support and executive information systems to comb through data and identify key trends. The information security field has encountered the same challenges; however, currently only rudimentary solutions are available. One reason for this is that the problem is more complicated and harder to address in the security space than it has been in previous addressed spaces.

Future products must collect raw data from industry-leading vendors and correlate this information to identify critical patterns in your information security environment. Visualization of these patterns will enable your staff to understand and address threats to your environment more quickly.

Other industries such as petrochemicals have automated controls to manage their business and take actions, including turning off the flow of oil when a pipeline breaks. The information security industry needs to catch up in this area because remediation steps must occur in minutes or even seconds after an incident to mitigate the impact to your operations.

Security Solution Evolution

Takings these trends one step further, here we provide a general overview of the current and future technologies. These solutions span security for the gateway/ server/client, applications security, and overall management of your information security program. Figure 8-5 provides a summary of these solutions.

Security Solution Evolution

	Client/Server/ Gateway	Application Security	Security Management
Tomorrow	Client Compliance	Application Intrusion Prevention	Cross Product Correlation
	Automated Lockdown		
	Automated Patching	Correlated Application Intrusion Prevention	Adaptive Management
	Virus Throttling	Application Lockdown	Automated Lockdown
			Multi-Vendor
Today	Signatures	Database Vulnerability Scanners	Multi-Product, Single Vendor
	Anomaly Detection		
	Router Throttling	Application Specific Protection	Single Product Manageability
	Intrusion Prevention		

Figure 8-5   Solution evolution.

Gateway/Server/Client Security—Today

Existing technology relies upon two major methods for protection: *signatures* and *anomaly detection*. Signatures identify an attack or suspicious file based upon a known differentiating property. A header section of an email message with the words "I Love You" identified a virus with the same name. Signatures are effective due to the speed and low incidence of false positives.

The shortcoming of signatures is that attackers can modify attacks or files so that they can bypass your protection. For example, if the header of the I Love You Virus were changed to "We Love You," the virus would avoid detection. Other solutions also use *signature recognition* including intrusion detection tools, which face the same challenge when an intruder modifies his attack (commonly referred to as a variant) to bypass protection. In addition, signatures only provide protection against known threats that security vendors have analyzed and that have differentiating properties.

Anomaly detection identifies patterns that deviate from what's considered normal. The financial services industry, for example, is able to detect credit card fraud through anomalies in usage, such as a sudden change in the location of charges or pattern of purchases. Requests for Comments (RFCs) dictate the structure and format of many TCP/IP protocols, and deviations from these RFCs are an example of what anomaly detection can identify.

Heuristics are a form of anomaly detection. They operate in a similar fashion, using a number of techniques to examine files, review network traffic, and analyze other activities in your computing environment to determine whether something is going wrong. Anti-virus products commonly use this technique to identify possibly malicious code. They can operate in a *static mode*, waiting for patterns to appear, or *dynamic mode,* where heuristic scanners test files in a controlled environment to determine whether they are malicious. Some security products also use both anomaly detection and heuristics to detect some forms of network reconnaissance by hackers, including post scanning, and DoS attacks.

Anomaly detection and heuristics are problematic because it's difficult to evaluate all the possible patterns without creating many false alarms, or *false positives,* that your staff must then investigate. The possible patterns also change on a regular basis, and this evaluation must be done at high speeds that require considerable computing power.

Router throttling limits the data or *packets* that the network sends through routers during an outbreak. Your staff could preconfigure routers to forward a limited number of packets during specific outbreak conditions, thus slowing down an attack. The idea here is to slow things down and give your security staff time to investigate what's happening by limiting the amount of information entering and leaving your computing infrastructure.

Intrusion prevention is emerging as the new proactive solution, combining the proactive protection of vulnerability management tools with the reactive protection of intrusion detection tools. Instead of just alerting someone that a possible intrusion has taken place, these tools will automatically take action to minimize potential damage. Intrusion prevention systems can also operate proactively with vulnerability management tools, changing system configurations to eliminate vulnerabilities. Intrusion prevention will be essential in the future because new threats will move quickly, and human response will no longer be possible.

Client/Server/Gateway Security—Tomorrow

Future technology must shift toward a proactive solution; we've provided an overview of a few of these areas here. *Client compliance* will validate that any machine connecting to an organization's network is complying with security policies, such as having updated virus definitions, complying with personal firewall rules, updated patches, and so on. If a client is not in compliance, it's restricted to specific parts of the network where the user can update his machine to adhere to the specific security policy. One technical challenge in this area is handling clients that are not yet running *client compliancy software*.

Automated lockdown gives your company the ability to lock down critical portions of its infrastructure during an outbreak. For example, this might include limiting access to your mission-critical systems until someone has investigated the potential issue or automatically blocking email attachments during an outbreak. Security personnel often limit access to a building while an investigation is underway or during an incident, and this is an electronic version of that process.

Automated patching enables your organization to download, install, and fix security vulnerabilities without manual intervention. This capability exists today for some clients; however, automated patching for servers and gateway devices is much more problematic because of the need to restart the devices to complete patch installation. For mission-critical systems and gateway devices that must always be available, this is a major problem. These servers often run specialized applications that your staff must test thoroughly to ensure that the patch does not "break" the application functionality. This makes automated patch management difficult.

Virus throttling slows down the computer-to-computer communication attempts from an infected system to other systems, thereby slowing down the propagation of the virus. This technology is reactive in nature and can help buy time to remediate vulnerable systems. This technology can be effective to prevent or slow the spread of blended threats such as Nimda and Slammer.

These are a few examples of how security technology will mature over the next couple of years to address future threats. *Application security*, which is quite immature when compared to the client/server/gateway security area, is reviewed next.

Application Security—Today

Another major challenge in the future involves application security, as companies rely heavily on e-commerce to conduct business. The major issue here is that until recently, vendors designed business applications for use by company employees, and outside parties used them on a limited basis. However, modern e-commerce exposes these applications directly to the Internet for use by customers and partners. Information security technology hasn't kept pace with this migration, which poses a risk to your company. Refer to Figure 8-6 for a graphic example of application security challenges.

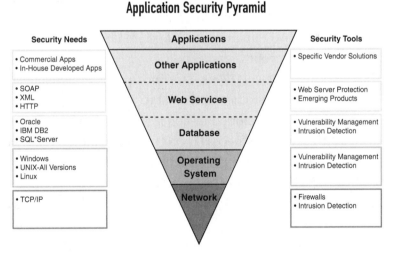

Figure 8-6 Application security pyramid.

At the bottom of the pyramid, you have well-known standards, and security vendors have developed solutions to protect these areas. As you move up the pyramid, security needs grow exponentially because standards are more recent, current standards don't apply, or the industry hasn't established them yet. Security solutions have not kept pace with the requirements in these areas.

Starting at the bottom of the pyramid, you have the network with TCP/IP for transferring information. The Internet Engineering Task Force (IETF) has established standards in this area, in addition to many vendors' proprietary standards, and firewalls and intrusion detection tools can provide protection to ensure that only authorized messages conforming to these standards can enter or leave your environment.

Moving up the pyramid, only a few operating systems control the majority of the market, and once again, security solutions are available to address potential issues. These include vulnerability management and intrusion detection. Best practices also exist to ensure that your staff hardens the operating system by using recommended configurations and applying vendor-supplied patches.

The final section of the pyramid represents applications, and it is composed of three areas: *database, web services,* and *other applications.* Three vendors offer the majority of database products today, and once again, vulnerability management and intrusion detection solutions are available to address most threats in this area. The two remaining sections are large, complex areas that pose a significant threat to your organization.

We will start with *other applications.* This includes commercially available software such as ERP and customer relationship management (CRM) systems, in addition to applications developed in-house. Due to the lack of standards and immaturity of this area, it's necessary to purchase individual security products to protect these systems, provided that these solutions exist.

Because of the broad nature of this area, it's quite possible that you will not have security products for either your commercial solutions or systems developed in-house. In these cases, look for solutions that protect the technology upon which these applications are based. If you developed an application using Lotus Notes, you should find security products that work with it because they are more likely to be compatible with your applications.

As depicted in Figure 8-6, this area is quite large, and even small companies might have 20 or more applications that they need to protect.

Web Services

Web services using XML and SOAP are not currently in widespread use; however, this area is getting considerable attention. Some organizations are deploying these applications, and your information security program needs to address this area. Security requirements in this area include support for the following protocols:

- **SOAP**—Simple Object Access Protocol used by web services for messaging

- **XML**—Extensible Mark-up Language, which is an extension of HTML used to develop web applications today

- **HTTP**—Hypertext Transfer Protocol used by Internet web browsers today

Early versions of standards for these protocols are currently available; however, vendors are generally reluctant to ensure that their products are in compliance before final standards are available.

The challenge for security organizations is that few security products are able to examine web services messages, such as SOAP, and determine whether they are valid. This is due to security standards only recently approved, in addition to the reluctance of security vendors to invest before the standards are finalized.

For example, a proxy firewall operates by reading a message, validating that the message conforms to certain standards, and then rewriting the message. In the case of web services, most firewalls do not know how to examine SOAP messages. These messages will pass right through your firewalls without the firewall checking for attacks.

Although early versions of security solutions for web services are starting to appear, application-level security is the next security frontier. Unfortunately, technology is playing catch-up here.

Application Security—Tomorrow

Application intrusion prevention and *application lockdown* are examples of future application security technology. Application intrusion prevention will extend intrusion prevention capabilities to applications. These capabilities are currently only available at the network and operating system level, although early versions of some products are starting to appear.

Correlated application intrusion prevention would extend this protection across multiple applications such as ERP and CRM systems. If an attack occurs in one of these systems, it would alert other systems, which would immediately begin to take their own preventative measures.

Application lockdown could include shutting down access to a system if security products discover a network attack in progress or denying all queries to the system if one malicious query is attempting to access confidential information such as credit card numbers. This is similar to the automated lockdown described in gateway/server/client solutions, and it operates in the same manner.

Security Management—Today

Management is the ability to get all your security products working together in an orchestrated fashion. Currently, security products operate independently and require considerable human intervention to protect your business effectively.

Security consoles are currently available that provide summary information for a particular security device. Some of these consoles can manage a few of the products from a single vendor such as anti-virus and firewalls and enable your staff to perform this function from a central location.

Early versions of applications that are able to manage products from more than one vendor are appearing on the market. This is quite important because few companies currently rely upon a single vendor for all their security needs.

Security Management—Tomorrow

The future of information security will rest upon the ability of organizations to address management issues. All these tools must work in a coordinated fashion to protect your business from complex, rapidly spreading threats. Three areas for future development include *correlation, adaptive management*, and *automated lockdown*.

Cross product correlation is extending management to include all the security products that protect your organization. Your company might have anti-virus software, firewalls, and vulnerability management tools. The goal is to manage all of them together. These products must integrate well and respond quickly when one device, such as a firewall, detects an attack, working in harmony to protect the business. In the future, human response will not be possible when threats can spread in minutes or seconds.

The idea behind adaptive management and lockdown is to build systems in which various security components within your enterprise communicate using a centralized management system and coordinate their response during an attack.

Suppose that a client machine's intrusion detection component detects an attack from a specific machine. The target machine could note the address of the attacker's machine and alert its client firewall to block all traffic from that address. The attacked computer could then alert the central management system, which in turn could instruct all network clients to block traffic from the attacker.

Automated lockdown could include automatically blocking attachments or blocking traffic at a firewall during an outbreak. The management system would initiate lockdown, and the system could detect a breach of the firewall and lock down all desktops. In the future, we might see a distributed reasoning system that would allow for cross-network communication and correlation of events and subsequent lockdown as appropriate.

Underlying all these technologies is the need for unified central management systems. These systems must be capable of managing the various security technologies in an organization, in addition to aggregating information across all these technologies. Management systems would serve as the control center for the information security program, constantly monitoring the environment for suspicious behaviors and reacting quickly. Management and application security are the cornerstones of future information security technology and are areas in which considerable investments will be made.

One of the areas receiving considerable effort for security management is dashboards. Dashboards are visualizations tools that show metrics in real-time for different levels of security management personnel. The goal is to help security management personnel effectively drive their efforts on a near real-time basis. These dashboards rely upon the effective aggregation, normalization, and correlation of data from a wide spectrum of security devices. These tools are no different from your automobile's dashboard that provides you with all the information necessary to assist in your driving decisions.

View into the Future Summary

This chapter provided some insight into future threats and trends for the information security industry. Threats will become more complex and will spread faster, and companies will need to put programs in place to address these issues. Future threats were covered, in addition to the possibility of these threats expanding beyond businesses to cause major disruptions in basic infrastructure including power, water, and communications.

The information security industry needs simple, easier-to-manage solutions. Lack of these solutions is a reflection of an immature market. Improved solutions will appear in the near future. Business executives need to evaluate how these threats could affect their future strategies and plan accordingly.

Key Points for This Chapter

- Future security threats will be more complex, and their impacts will extend from individuals and organizations to regions and the entire globe.

- Threats will also spread much more quickly, from the minutes that it took the Slammer Worm to spread to seconds in the future.

- Zero-day threats, whereby a hacker creates and releases an attack without advance notice, will occur in the future and provide additional challenges to your information security program.

- Hacker intentions will shift from notoriety (such as defacing a web site) to organized crime and terrorist organizations that are focused on money or public disruption.

- Industry solutions will need to shift to proactive security because it will no longer be possible for people to respond in time to future attacks.

- Security management will also become important to ensure that all the components of your information security program work together to respond to future attacks.

- The security industry will need to adapt solutions from other industries such as oil and gas with control systems that react automatically to events such as pipeline leaks.

Chapter 9

Summary

One of Britain's oldest financial institutions collapsed in 1995 from unauthorized trades that lost the firm more than $1 billion (£830 million). This was a story of financial risk management gone wrong that brought down Britain's oldest merchant bank, which financed Napoleonic wars, the Louisiana purchase, and the Erie Canal. This collapse can be traced to a single trader located in a small office in Singapore.

This trader made a name for himself by cleaning up a back office mess in the company's Jakarta office. He then applied for a position in the Singapore office and was named general manager with authority to hire both traders and back office staff. He took the necessary exam so that he could also trade but began making unauthorized speculative trades, hiding all of this in an unused error account. He lost money from the beginning and increased his bets, only to lose more money, while keeping the company management unaware of these activities. He was accomplished at fraud and falsified records and made up stories to deflect questions from management and auditors. While he was secretly accumulating losses, he was publicly recording profits and held a celebrity status within the firm.

He was finally caught and sentenced to six and a half years in Singapore's Changi prison, but his company was not able to survive these losses and no longer exists. This final chapter outlines key points that executives should understand regarding information security and how to prevent a similar experience at their organizations.

Introduction

This chapter is for the executive who flips to the last page of a presentation looking for the punch line or recommendations. This chapter is the punch line for this book, and it covers the high-level topics that executives need to understand.

Overview

This chapter provides a list of strategies that your company should consider for improving your information security program. These include the 10 essential components of an effective information security program. Executives should become familiar with these recommendations and consider incorporating them into their future business strategies.

Ten Essential Components for a Successful Information Security Program

This section provides a quick overview of key information security concepts and suggestions on how to implement them at your company. These suggestions follow the consistent themes of people, process, and technology used throughout this book.

1—CEO "Owns" Information Security Program

The CEO needs to assume overall ownership of the information security program and set the tone for the rest of the organization. The CEO's staff should be involved in developing broad objectives for the program, and the CEO should conduct regular reviews to ensure that his staff is meeting the program goals. The CEO must consider information security an essential component of the company's business strategy and a key enabler for successful business operations. The potential effect of information security issues on revenue streams, customer satisfaction, and brand are too great to ignore.

Too often, executives relegate information security to the information security staff that don't have the authority to implement changes that might be necessary for a successful program. Unless the executive staff considers information security an important component of your business strategy, the pressure to offer new products and services will overshadow the program. The information security organization can manage the program; however, active involvement and support from the CEO and his staff are essential for success.

2—Assign Senior-Level Staff Responsibility for Information Security

You should assign a senior-level staff member responsibility for the information security program at your company. Depending upon the size of your organization, this individual might be responsible for this area alone, or she might have many other responsibilities, too. Ideally, this individual should report directly to the CEO or COO and have the authority to carry out this role within the company.

Whenever possible, it's advisable to have a full-time information security organization staffed with experienced information security professionals. It is difficult to perform this function on a part-time basis because the industry is changing at a rapid pace. Placing inexperienced or part-time staff in this role will increase the probability of a security incident affecting your business operations. Smaller organizations should consider managed services vendors because they can offer the necessary expertise and scale for your business operations.

3—Establish a Cross-Functional Information Security Governance Board

Establishment of a cross-functional information security governance board is necessary to ensure the success of your program. Your information security program will place restrictions on how you conduct your business. It is also important that your processes incorporate the requirements of multiple organizations.

Internal restrictions include employee policies on appropriate use of computers that will require HR involvement. External restrictions will include compliance with industry regulations and local laws to ensure that your company is conducting business appropriately. Remember that when you conduct business on the Internet, you are doing business on a worldwide basis.

This board needs to be responsible for establishing the appropriate security policies within the company in addition to enforcing these policies within their respective organizations. The governance board should be held accountable for the success of the program and should not rely entirely upon the information security organization.

4—Establish Metrics to Manage the Program

The first step for improving any process is measurement, and your information security program is no different. You should establish clear goals and hold your information security organization accountable for achieving them. It's important to establish a set of metrics to measure the effectiveness of your information security program and regularly review them with executive staff. For benchmarking examples, see the Information Security Forum (www.securityforum.com).

Benchmarking with other companies within your industry can help highlight the effectiveness of your program. Security-conscious industries such as financial services must meet much more stringent criteria before they can consider their programs successful. Whenever possible, it's advisable to drive toward *quantitative* metrics to evaluate your program because *qualitative* measures are less meaningful.

5—Implement Ongoing Security Improvement Program

You should view information security as a *journey,* not a destination. Researchers identify new threats on a daily basis, and your information security program needs to address these threats. You need to follow the information security life cycle of measure, improve, and manage to ensure the success of your program.

Continuous improvement programs are common in industries such as manufacturing, and the same concepts apply to information security. The natural tendency is for a program to stagnate, but stagnation leads to problems. In addition, if your organization is constantly in *fire fighting* mode, you might be too focused on tactical areas and might not have an adequate improvement plan in place.

6—Conduct Independent Reviews of Your Information Security Program

Regular oversight and independent review of your information security program is important. No matter how efficiently you think your information security program is operating, it is important to have a third party's validation. These assessments are no different from financial audits and require the same discipline to be successful.

Review the results of these audits with executive staff and the individuals who are responsible for resolution of issues. Cooperation of information security staff is essential. The employees should not consider the reviews a witch-hunt to ensure that they're doing their jobs correctly; instead, they are key components of an effective information security program. Pay particular attention to the ongoing trends of these reviews to ensure that the program is improving over time and that the same issues are not recurring.

7—Layer Security at Gateway, Server, and Client

The advent of *blended threats* that attack multiple components of your computing infrastructure has raised the bar on information security requirements. Companies can no longer rely upon firewalls at their Internet connections to protect their computing infrastructure. They now need to have multiple layers of defense. You must deploy information security technology at the gateways that separate your enterprise from the outside world, on servers that your staff shares, and on individual computers or *clients*.

These three layers of defense are required to protect your business from more complex threats that will evolve in the future. The third layer of defense at the client will also protect personnel who use mobile computers because they can't rely upon the protection of the company's security products when they are away from the office. Management of these multiple defense layers places an additional burden on the information security staff, but you cannot avoid it.

8—Separate Your Computing Environment into "Zones"

You also need to separate your enterprise-computing environment into *zones* that give your customers, partners, and employees the appropriate level of access to your systems. You can think of these zones as rings around your electronic business, with the outermost rings or zones accessible by your customers and partners. They will need to access your web site to learn more about your products and to engage in electronic commerce.

The next zone provides greater security and allows only your employees to access internal systems to conduct their jobs. Finally, your mission-critical systems are at the center of your electronic business. You will allow only a small number of employees to access these systems. You will deploy increasing levels of security and associated technology at each successive zone within your environment. You can think of this in the same context as a bank that has successive locks on the doors and finally a vault to secure valuables.

9—Start with Basics and Improve the Program

Information security programs can take years to implement, so it's important to start with the basics and continuously improve the program. From a technology perspective, this means starting with basic access controls and incrementally adding additional protection. From here, you can progress to the use of firewalls to protect your connections to the Internet or gateways and anti-virus software to protect your systems from malicious software.

It doesn't make sense to deploy some of the more advanced technology such as intrusion detection software unless you have addressed basics such as firewalls because you will be building your program on a poor foundation. Your program should include a roadmap that outlines how you will deploy the technology component over time. This approach will ensure that you are implementing the appropriate technology according to the benefits that you expect to achieve.

10—Consider Information Security an Essential Investment for Your Organization

Investments in information security should be considered along with all other major investments that are competing for scarce resources. Security risk analysis should be performed to determine the priorities for your program and appropriate levels of investment. This process starts by inventorying the critical assets within your organization and assessing the impact should these assets not be available for a period of time. Threats to these assets should be considered next, along with an analysis of how vulnerable your assets are to these threats. Finally, determining the likelihood of these threats occurring will enable you to complete your security risk analysis.

Business executives then need to review the results of this security risk analysis and determine the appropriate level of investment in your program. There are no easy answers here; this process requires a careful review of your company's critical assets and determines the impacts to your business should they become unavailable for a period of time.

Essential Components Summary

This chapter provided an overview of the key concepts that you should consider in your information security program. You should consider this chapter a shortcut that you can use to evaluate your program quickly. Other chapters contain detailed information that explains these concepts in more detail.

Appendix A
Security Evaluation Framework

The security evaluation framework that was described in the book is also included in this appendix and can be used at your company. You may choose to tailor these templates to your company and industry because it is important to have a security program that meets your future business requirements.

Information Security Business Dependency Matrix

Component	Ratings (High - 3, Medium - 2, Low - 1)
Company Characteristics	
■ Dependence upon systems to offer products and services to customers	
■ Value of company's intellectual property stored in electronic form	
■ Requirement for 24-7 business systems	
■ Degree of change within company (expansions, M&A, new markets)	
■ Business size (number of offices, number of customers, level of revenue) and complexity (processes, systems, products)	
Industry Characteristics	
■ Budget for security administration and security initiatives	
■ Potential impact to national or critical infrastructure	
■ Customer sensitivity to security and privacy	
■ Level of industry regulation regarding security (GLBA, HIPAA)	
■ Brand or revenue impact of security incident	
■ Extent of business operations dependent upon third parties (partners, suppliers)	
■ Customers' ability to quickly switch vendors based upon their ability to offer services in a secure manner	
Average Overall Ranking (Total Scores/12)	

Information Security People Evaluation Template

Component	Score (0–2)	Comments
Strategy		
■ Written information security strategy		
■ Strategy updated on regular basis		
■ Proactive versus reactive organization		
■ Minimal impacts to business operations due to security issues		
■ Industry compliance issues (for example, HIPAA) have been addressed		
■ Industry certifications (for example, BS 7799) have been achieved		
Components		
■ Qualified leader (for example, CISSP) of organization		
■ Experienced staff with necessary training		
■ Dedicated information security staff		
■ One staff per 1,000 personnel		
■ Ongoing training program in place		
Administration		
■ Function provides regular status reports to executive staff and board of directors		
■ Executive staff own the information security program		
■ Active engagement with critical functions such as human resources and legal		
■ Authority to enforce information security program		
■ Segregation of duties		
■ Perform risk analysis and management (assessments, audits, and compliance)		
Total Score (0–34)		

Information Security Future People Architecture Template

Component	Current Score (0–2)	Desired Future Score (0–2)	Priority (High, Medium, Low)	Desired Time Frame	Comments
Strategy					
■ Written information security strategy					
■ Strategy updated on regular basis					
■ Proactive versus reactive organization					
■ Minimal impacts to business operations due to security issues					
■ Industry compliance issues for example, HIPAA) have been addressed					
■ Industry certifications (for example, BS 7799) have been achieved					
Components					
■ Qualified leader (for example, CISSP) of organization					
■ Experienced staff with necessary training					
■ Dedicated information security staff					
■ One staff per 1,000 personnel					
■ Ongoing training program in place					
Administration					
■ Function provides regular status reports to executive staff and board of directors					
■ Executive staff owns the information security program					
■ Active engagement with critical functions such as human resources and legal					
■ Authority to enforce information security program					
■ Perform risk analysis and management (assessments, audits, and compliance)					
Total Score (0–34)					

Information Security Process Evaluation Template

Component	Score (0–2)	Comments
Strategy		
■ Written policies in consistent and easy-to-read format		
■ Easily accessible via company intranet		
■ Up to date with relevant changes		
■ Nontechnical and easy to understand		
■ Broad policies that cover relevant topics		
■ Incorporate risk analysis and management		
Components		
■ Account administration		
■ Remote access		
■ Vulnerability management		
■ Security awareness		
■ Emergency response		
■ Acceptable use of computers, email, Internet		
Administration		
■ Consistent application across company		
■ Details on how policies will be monitored and enforced		
■ Active involvement of critical functions such as human resources and legal in creation of policies		
■ Multiple communication methods to disseminate policy changes		
■ Executive staff approval of policies		
Total Score (0–34)		

Information Security Future Process Architecture Template

Component	Current Score (0–2)	Desired Future Score (0–2)	Priority (High, Medium, Low)	Desired Time Frame	Comments
Strategy					
■ Written policies in consistent and easy-to-read format					
■ Easily accessible via company intranet					
■ Up to date with relevant changes					
■ Nontechnical and easy to understand					
■ Broad policies that cover relevant topics					
■ Incorporate risk analysis and management					
Components					
■ Account administration					
■ Remote access					
■ Vulnerability management					
■ Security awareness					
■ Emergency response					
■ Acceptable use of computers, email, Internet					
Administration					
■ Consistent application across company					
■ Details on how policies will be monitored and enforced					
■ Active involvement of critical functions such as human resources and legal in creation of policies					
■ Multiple communication methods to disseminate policy changes					
■ Executive staff approval of policies					
Total Score (0–34)					

Information Security Asset Inventory Example

Asset	Category	Location	Comments
Client			
■ Executive staff computers	■ Critical	■ Headquarters	■ Detailed inventory developed
■ Employee computers	■ Standard	■ Worldwide	■ Only high-level inventory
■ Personal digital assistants	■ Standard	■ Worldwide	■ Unable to establish inventory
Server			
■ ERP	■ Mission-Critical	■ Headquarters	■ Detailed inventory developed
■ CRM	■ Mission-Critical	■ Headquarters	■ Detailed inventory developed
■ E-commerce	■ Mission-Critical	■ Headquarters	■ Detailed inventory developed
■ Departmental	■ Standard	■ Worldwide	■ High-level inventory only
Gateway			
■ Customer DMZ	■ Mission-Critical	■ Major geographic regions	■ Very detailed inventory
■ Partner DMZ	■ Mission-Critical	■ Major geographic regions	■ Very detailed inventory
■ Email	■ Critical	■ Major geographic regions	■ Very detailed inventory
■ Internet	■ Standard	■ Major geographic regions	■ Very detailed inventory

Information Security Risk Assessment Summary Example

Asset	Category	Major Threats	Vulnerabilities	Risk Assessment
Client				
▪ Executive staff computers	▪ Critical	▪ Theft	▪ Security awareness	▪ Medium
▪ Employee computers	▪ Standard	▪ Viruses	▪ Virus definition update process	▪ Low
▪ Personal digital assistants	▪ Standard	▪ Theft	▪ Security awareness	▪ Low
Servers				
▪ ERP, CRM	▪ Mission-Critical	▪ Impersonation	▪ Account administration process	▪ High
▪ E-commerce	▪ Mission-Critical	▪ Hacking	▪ Patch management	▪ Medium
▪ Email	▪ Critical	▪ Viruses	▪ Virus definition update process	▪ Low
▪ Departmental	▪ Standard	▪ Social engineering	▪ Security awareness	▪ Low
Gateway				
▪ Customer–partner DMZ	▪ Mission-Critical	▪ Denial of service	▪ Overall security architecture	▪ High
▪ Email	▪ Critical	▪ Viruses	▪ Virus definition update process	▪ Low
▪ Internet	▪ Standard	▪ Impersonation	▪ Account administration process	▪ Low

Information Security Technology Evaluation Template

Component	Score (0–2)	Comments
Strategy		
■ Comprehensive information security architecture		
■ Computing environment segmented into security zones		
■ Security layered at gateway, server, and client		
■ Security roadmap includes both strategic and tactical objectives		
■ Strategy supports current models for conducting business		
Components		
■ AAA		
■ Anti-virus		
■ Firewalls		
■ Vulnerability management		
■ Intrusion detection		
Administration		
■ Regular scanning and remediation program		
■ Quarterly penetration testing		
■ Annual independent audit of security program		
■ Regular update of anti-virus definitions		
■ Change management		
■ Reporting on security incidents and initiatives to executive management and board of directors		
Total Score (0–32)		

Information Security Future Technology Architecture Template

Component	Current Score (0–2)	Desired Future Score (0–2)	Priority (High, Medium, Low)	Desired Time Frame	Comments
Strategy					
■ Comprehensive information security architecture					
■ Computing environment segmented into security zones					
■ Security layered at gateway, server, and client					
■ Security roadmap includes both strategic and tactical objectives					
■ Strategy supports current models for conducting business					
Components					
■ AAA					
■ Anti-virus					
■ Firewalls					
■ Vulnerability management					
■ Intrusion detection					
Administration					
■ Regular scanning and remediation program					
■ Quarterly penetration testing					
■ Annual independent audit of security program					
■ Regular update of anti-virus definitions					
■ Change management					
■ Reporting on security incidents and initiatives to executive management and board of directors					
Total Score (0–32)					

Information Security Existing Program Evaluation Summary Example

Program Component	Score	Comments
People		
■ Strategy	7	■ No formal strategy exists today
■ Components	8	■ Staff focused on day-to-day firefighting
■ Administration	9	■ Minimal involvement of executive staff
People Score	**24**	
Process		
■ Strategy	10	■ Informal policies that are not followed consistently
■ Components	9	■ Policies are not easily accessed by employees
■ Administration	7	■ All major security policies have been considered in program
Process Score	**26**	
Technology		
■ Strategy	6	■ No technology architecture is in place, and changes are tactical in nature
■ Components	10	■ Major technology components have been deployed
■ Administration	10	■ Informal program to protect environments from security threats
Technology Score	**26**	
Overall Average Rating (0–100)	**76**	

Information Security Business Dependency Matrix Example

Component	Ratings (High - 3, Medium - 2, Low - 1)
Company Characteristics	
■ Dependence upon systems to offer products and services to customers	2
■ Value of company's intellectual property stored in electronic form	2
■ Requirement for 24-7 business systems	3
■ Degree of change within company (expansions, M&A, new markets)	1
■ Business size (number of offices, number of customers, level of revenue) and complexity (processes, systems, products)	1
Industry Characteristics	
■ Budget for security administration and security initiatives	1
■ Potential impact to national or critical infrastructure	1
■ Customer sensitivity to security and privacy	3
■ Level of industry regulation regarding security (GLBA, HIPAA)	1
■ Brand or revenue impact of security incident	3
■ Extent of business operations dependent upon third parties (partners, suppliers)	2
■ Customers' ability to quickly switch vendors based upon their ability to offer services in a secure manner	3
Average Overall Ranking (Total Score/12)	2

Information Security Program Assessment Scoring

Business Dependency	Program Rating	Overall Assessment
High	95–100	Good
	90–94	Average
	Below 90	Poor
Medium	90–100	Good
	80–89	Average
	Below 80	Poor
Low	85–100	Good
	70–84	Average
	Below 70	Poor

Information Security Gap Analysis Example

Component	Current Score (0–2)	Desired Future Score (0–2)	Priority (High, Medium, Low)	Desired Time Frame	Comments
People					
■ Strategy	7	12	High	12 months	■ No formal strategy exists today
■ Components	8	10	Medium	18 months	■ Staff focused on day-to-day firefighting
■ Administration	9	10	Low	24 months	■ Minimal involvement of executive staff
People Summary	24	32			
Process					
■ Strategy	10	12	High	12 months	■ Informal policies that are not followed consistently
■ Components	9	12	Low	24 months	■ Policies are not easily accessed by employees
■ Administration	7	8	Low	18 months	■ All major security policies have been considered in program
Process Summary	26	30			
Technology					
■ Strategy	6	8	Medium	12 months	■ No technology architecture is in place, and changes are tactical in nature
■ Components	10	10	Low	24 months	■ Major technology components have been deployed
■ Administration	10	10	Low	24 months	■ Informal program to protect environments from security threats
Technology Summary	26	28			
Total Score (0–100)	76	90			

Information Security Strategic Alternatives Example

Alternative		Time Frame	Estimated Costs	Benefits
Aggressive implementation	■ Hire third-party integrator to accelerate information security implementation ■ Create CISO position and hire experienced leader ■ Establish corporate governance board to oversee program	6–12 months	$5–10 million	■ Continue e-commerce initiative ■ $4 million revenue opportunity
Accelerated implementation	■ Hire third party to assist in information security program implementation ■ Create separate information security organization and hire experienced leader ■ Provide management team with regular updates on program	12–18 months	$3–5 million	■ Delay e-commerce initiative ■ $2 million revenue opportunity
Incremental improvements	■ Leverage third parties in selected areas ■ Establish training program for information security staff ■ Formalize program and provide regular updates on progress	18–24 months	$1–2 million	■ Postpone e-commerce initiative ■ No revenue opportunity

Information Security Roadmap Example

Component	Strategic Initiatives	Time Frame	Tactical Plans	Time Frame
People	■ Develop information security strategy	6 months	■ Assign acting manager for department	30 days
	■ Create and staff separate information security organization	12 months	■ Clarify roles and responsibilities for information security	60 days
	■ Establish formal training program to receive industry-recognized credentials	24 months	■ Schedule firewall training for all staff	90 days
Processes	■ Establish corporate governance board with key members of management team	9 months	■ Collect existing security policies	30 days
	■ Publish security policies on company intranet	9 months	■ Develop consistent format for policies	90 days
	■ Establish company-wide security awareness program	18 months	■ Engage with human resources and legal on existing policies	90 days
Technology	■ Establish technology architecture	12 months	■ Scan environment and remedy high vulnerabilities	90 days
	■ Provide regular reporting on effectiveness of program	18 months	■ Update virus definitions for all employees	30 days
	■ Have independent third-party audit program	12 months	■ Document changes to computing infrastructure	90 days

Information Security Project Template Example

<table>
<tr>
<td colspan="2">**Project: E-Commerce Site Security**</td>
<td>**Project Review Dates**
Last: July 1, 2004
This: Aug 1, 2004
Next: Sept 1, 2004</td>
</tr>
<tr>
<td colspan="2" rowspan="2">**Strategy: Address short-term issues with securing the e-commerce site**</td>
<td>**IT Project Owner:** Applicaions Director</td>
</tr>
<tr>
<td>**Customer/Department:** Sales and Marketing</td>
</tr>
<tr>
<td colspan="2">

Results Last 30 Days
- Updated the security patches for hardware supporting the e-commerce site
- Established regular monitoring program to manually monitor site and ensure it is functioning properly

Plans Next 30 Days
- Evaluate automated monitoring tools
- Complete interview process and hire additional security staff

Items for Attention
- Major software upgrade required in future

</td>
<td></td>
</tr>
</table>

Project Milestones	Data	Status	Budget	Amount
• Patch hardware and software	July 1	100%	• Consulting	$100K
• Manual monitoring process	July 1	100%	• Hardware	$200K
• Hire additional security staff	Aug 1	50%	• Software	$150K
• Automate monitoring process	Aug 1	50%		
• Upgrade to new e-commerce software	Sept 1	25%		
• Train marketing staff on new processes	Sept 1	25%		

Appendix B

Information Security Web Sites

The web sites listed in this appendix are excellent sources of information to improve your information security program. Much of this information is offered free of charge, and suggestions provided can be quickly implemented at your organization.

Government

- Department of Homeland Security—www.dhs.gov/dhspublic/
- U.S. National Infrastructure Protection Center—www.nipc.gov
- Federal Bureau of Investigation—www.fbi.gov
- National Security Institute—www.nsi.org

Education

- Cerias—Purdue University—www.cerias.purdue.edu

Information Security Industry

- Advanced Computing Systems Association—www.usenix.org/
- Common Vulnerabilities and Exposures—www.cve.mitre.org/

- Computer Emergency Response Team—www.cert.org/
- Computer Incident Advisory Capability—www.ciac.org/
- Computer Security Institute—www.gocsi.com
- CSO Online—www.csoonline.com/
- Electronic Frontier Foundation—www.eff.org
- Forum of Incident Response and Security (FIRST)—www.first.org
- High Technology Crimes Investigation Association (HTCIA)—www.htcia.org
- Incidents.org and Internet Storm Center—www.incidents.org
- Information Systems Security Association (ISSA)—www.issa.org
- Information Technology—Information Sharing and Analysis Center (IT-ISAC)—www.it.isac.org
- International Information Systems Security Certification Consortium (ISC)[2]—www.isc2.org
- Internet Society—www.isoc.org
- ITWorld.com—www.itworld.com/
- PacketStorm—packetstormsecurity.nl/
- Security Focus—www.securityfocus.com/
- Security Magazine—www.securitymagazine.com/
- Systems Administration, Networking, and Security Institute (SANS)—www.sans.org

Other

- Attrition.org—www.attrition.org/

Appendix C

Operational Security Standards

This appendix lists some operational standards that you might want to include in your security program. These standards are recognized worldwide and are excellent examples of industry best practices.

Government

- British Government—BSI security requirements (ISO 17700 and BS7799)— www.bsi-global.com
- General Accounting Office for U.S. Federal Government—Federal Information Systems Control Audit Methodology (FISCAM) requirements—www.gao.gov/ special.pubs/ai12.19.6.pdf
- Common Criteria IS15408 (Global Consortium), ISO promoted standard for security evaluation—niap.nist.gov/cc-scheme/defining-ccevs.html

Industry

- American Institute of Certified Public Accountants SysTrust requirements— www.aicpa.org
- Information Systems Security Association (ISSA)—Generally Accepted Information Security Principles (GAISP)—www.issa.org/gaisp.html

- Information Systems Audit and Control Association (ISACA) Control Objectives for Information and Related Technology (COBIT) requirements—www.isaca.org

- Center for Internet Security benchmarks for secure configurations—www.cisecurity.org

- SANs Top Twenty Internet security threats—www.sans.org/top20.htm

- Internet Engineering Task Force (IETF) Site Security Handbook (RFC 2196)—www.ietf.org

Business

- Visa's Digital Dozen for organizations that carry the Visa logo—usa.visa.com/business/merchants/cisp_requirements.html

Appendix D

Sample Security Job Descriptions

Job descriptions for the three major roles for an information security organization are provided in this appendix. These positions include information security director, information security analyst, and information security auditor. Depending upon the size of your organization, you might want to have multiple staff in these roles or a single individual assuming more than one role.

Information Security Director

Job Description

This position requires the ability to understand business issues and processes and to articulate the business context of projects and processes. A strong understanding of information security and software validation is required, and understanding of disaster recovery planning and business continuity process might be required. This person must be familiar with the principles and techniques of security risk analysis and must demonstrate an understanding of the management issues involved in implementing security processes and a security-aware culture in a large corporate environment.

Job Responsibilities

- Develop and implement information global security policies standards, and guidelines.

- Develop and implement a framework for security processes, roles, and responsibilities throughout the organization.

- Be capable of managing security requirements and a team of information security analysts.

- Develop technology solutions and processes that allow secure access to information assets.

- Participate in the system development cycle to ensure that security issues are taken into account and addressed early.

- Develop and enhance the skills and experience of both infrastructure and operational staff with specific security responsibilities to ensure that systems remain secure, available, and functional at all times.

- Ensure that information security is addressed as a business issue across the company and provide overall coordination and management of all security activities within the company.

- Coordinate information security training for employees, contractors, partners, and other third parties as appropriate.

- Monitor compliance with the organization's information security policies and procedures among employees, contractors, partners, and other third parties; resolve potential issues as needed.

- Perform information security risk assessments.

- Serve as information security consultant.

- Prepare the organization's disaster recovery and business continuity plans for information systems.

- Monitor changes in legislation and accreditation standards that affect information security.

Skill Requirements

- BA/BS degree in a technical area with 12+ years IS/IT experience, including at least 5 years of full-time information security background.

- Must be a Certified Information Systems Security Professional (CISSP, https://www.isc2.org/cgi/content.cgi?category=19), (ISC)^2 (https://www.isc2.org/cgi-bin/index.cgi) or Certified Information Security Manager (CISM,http://www.isaca.org/Template.cfm?Section=CISM_Certification&Template=/TaggedPage/TaggedPageDisplay.cfm&TPLID=16&ContentID=4528) from ISACA (http://www.isaca.org/).

- Strong communication and interpersonal skills.

- Strong knowledge of risk analysis and security techniques.

- Experience and understanding of TCP/IP open networking protocols is essential; knowledge of SSL/TLS and IPSec is required.

- Knowledge of DB2, Oracle, and SQL *Server would be an advantage.

- Knowledge of routers, switches, bridges, and wireless devices is required, as is knowledge of the communications architectures that link them together (for example, LANs, WANs, ISDN, PSTN, ATM, Frame Relay).

- Must have an understanding of the various types of firewall gateways and their design, configuration, and management.

- Knowledge of client-server technologies and systems.

- Knowledge of security and privacy requirements under GLB and HIPAA and international legislation when appropriate for your business (e.g., the European Union's Data Protection Directive, Canada's Personal Information Protection and Electronic Documents Act).

- Knowledge of SEI's CMMI (http://www.sei.cmu.edu/cmmi/) model.

Information Security Analyst

Job Description

This position will help formulate, define, and implement procedures that are necessary to ensure the safety of information systems assets, protecting them from intentional or inadvertent access or destruction. Will devise or modify systems or procedures to solve complex problems, balancing business needs against potential risks. Will interface with the user community to understand their privacy and security needs and will implement procedures and technologies to accommodate these requirements.

Job Responsibilities

- Implement global security policy, standards, guidelines, and procedures to ensure ongoing maintenance of security.

- Design and implement appropriate security controls to meet company security objectives.

- Monitor security by conducting periodic audits.

- Investigate security breaches, playing a lead role in working with legal matters associated with such breaches as necessary.

- Recommend security improvements by assessing current situations, evaluating trends, and anticipating requirements.

- Monitor and review Intrusion Detection Systems and firewall logs.

- Review firewall rulesets and router ACLs, and change requests for such.

- Perform network- and host-based vulnerability scans and penetration tests.

- Review and modify security policies for Intrusion Detection Systems and scanning tools.

- Identify, classify, and track information assets across the enterprise.

- Closely follow security-related trends, software, processes, laws, and regulations to provide strategy and tactics aligned with industry best practices.

Skill Requirements

- BA/BS degree in a technical area with 5+ years IS/IT experience, including *at least* 2 years of information security experience.

- Must have a Global Information Assurance Certification (http://www.giac.org/certifications.php) or vendor security-specific certification.

- Must have a detailed technical understanding of security point products (for example, various types of firewall gateways and their design, configuration, and management).

- Experience in conducting security vulnerability assessments, including experience with standard penetration testing, DoS, and virus attacking methods and tools used to isolate/monitor those attempts.

- Experience with switches and routers preferred.

- Technical expertise in core infrastructure and security (for example, Solaris, Windows, Cisco IOS, TCP/IP).

- Experience with troubleshooting during attempts/attacks in live production environments.

- Strong communication and interpersonal skills.

- Project management experience.

Information Security Auditor

Job Description

Evaluates and reports on the effectiveness of information security controls for information technology systems in accordance with the COSO (http://www.coso.org/) or other accepted frameworks and principles and internal/external audit policy to determine whether information systems processes and controls comply with generally accepted industry standards for information technology, regulatory requirements, and corporate policies and procedures. Has the ability to evaluate security controls within multiple processing environments (for example, Solaris and Windows). Performs general and application control reviews, information control reviews including system development standards, operating procedures, system security, e-business controls, programming controls including program code, telecommunications controls, business resumptions, and disaster recovery and system maintenance. Uses and develops appropriate software tools and techniques to discover cyber security vulnerabilities and subsequently validate weaknesses.

Job Responsibilities

- Directs, plans, organizes, and conducts information technology (IT) infrastructure audits, including management of information security, continuity of business systems, management of information technology assets, management of application programs, management of computer operations, management of networks, data management, technical architecture, and problem resolution to provide reasonable assurance to management of adherence to sound business practices and to offer constructive analysis and appraisal of company policies, procedures, financial and operational reports, system of internal controls, and efficiency of operations.

- Directs, plans, organizes, and conducts application audits of the company's business systems to provide reasonable assurance to management of adherence to sound business practices and to offer constructive analysis and appraisal of company policies, procedures, financial and operational reports, data integrity, system of internal controls, and efficiency of operations.

- Responsible for reviewing all audit work papers in conjunction with IT internal audits and projects prior to completion of audit.

- Determines the scope of assigned audits, identifies potential problem areas to be examined during the course of the audits, and prepares or updates audit plans and programs. All significant findings and recommendations will be communicated to corporate management and to the

Audit and Compliance Committee of the Board of Directors in timely and objective reports.

- Conducts IT departmental activities in accordance with the internal audit department charter.

- Reports to management conditions that pose an inordinate risk to the company. Also identifies areas where controls, operational efficiency, and cost effectiveness can be improved and makes recommendations for improvement to management.

- Works with all information systems departments to gain an understanding of their goals and responsibilities. Assists the departments in developing reliable controls over IT functions. Reviews existing controls to determine their effectiveness. Reviews all findings and recommendations that identify exceptions to company policy or sound business practice with appropriate IT management personnel. Also stays abreast of progress on IT audit issues.

Skill Requirements

- Bachelors degree in a technology-, audit-, or financial-related field.

- Minimum five years of experience in IT auditing or an equivalent combination of education and experience.

- Financial background sufficient to have a working knowledge of generally accepted accounting principles.

- Knowledge of IS technology and controls in multiple environments (for example, Oracle running on Solaris, Windows, client/server, Internet/intranet, telecommunications, e-business, and web-enabled systems/applications).

- Knowledge of information security and administrative controls in the previously noted environments.

- Understanding of computer programming and computer-assisted audit techniques. Prior programming experience with current programming languages is highly desirable.

- Ability to prepare programs to extract and analyze with the ability to use data analysis utilities such as SQL, Business Objects, and other query languages. Knowledge of JCL is desirable.

- Strong communication and interpersonal skills.

- Project management experience.

- Must be a Certified Information Security Manager (CISM) from ISACA, or GIAC IT Security Audit Essentials (GSAE) or GIAC Systems and Network Auditor (GSNA) certified.

Glossary

access

The ability to read, write, modify, or use any of a company's system resources.

access control

Prevention of unauthorized use of any of a company's system resources either externally (by an intruder) or internally (by an employee who should not have access).

accountability

Ensuring that activities on supported systems can be traced to an individual who is held responsible for the integrity of the data.

assurance

A level of confidence that the information system architecture mediates and enforces the organization's security policy.

audit trail

A documented record of events allowing an auditor (or security administrator) to reconstruct past system activities.

authenticate

To verify the identity of a user, device, or any other system entity.

authorization

Granting officially approved access rights to a user, process, or program in accordance with a company's security policy.

back door

Code that is specifically written into applications or operating systems to allow unauthorized access. Also called a *trap door*.

blended threat

Blended threats combine the characteristics of viruses, worms, Trojan horses, and malicious code with system and Internet vulnerabilities to initiate, transmit, and spread an attack. By using multiple methods and techniques, blended threats can rapidly spread and cause widespread damage.

buffer overflow

A buffer overflow is a type of programmatic flaw that is due to a programmer allowing for an unbounded operation on data. Buffer overflow conditions commonly occur during memory copy operations. In these cases, a lack of bounds checking can allow memory to be written beyond the buffer, corrupting potentially sensitive values in adjacent memory. Buffer overflow conditions have typically been exploited to hijack program execution flow (that is, execute arbitrary instructions) by overwriting activation records in stack memory. Buffer overflows in the heap have also proven exploitable, enabling attackers to have their own instructions executed in the process space of the affected program.

bulletin board

Enables users from the Internet to write or read messages posted by other users and to exchange programs and files.

compromise

Violation of a company's system security policy by an intruder. It can result in the modification, destruction, or theft of data.

computer crime

Any form of illegal act involving electronic information and computer equipment.

computer fraud

A computer crime that an intruder commits to obtain money or something of value from a company. Often, all traces of the crime are covered up. Computer fraud typically involves modification, destruction, theft, or disclosure of data.

confidentiality

Ensuring that sensitive data is limited to specific individuals (external and internal) or groups within an organization. The confidentiality of the information is based on the degree to which an organization must protect its information—for example, registered, proprietary, or nonproprietary.

conflict-of-interest escalation

A preset procedure for escalating a security incident if any members of the support or security teams are suspect.

contingency plan

A security plan to ensure that mission-critical computer resources are available to a company in the event of a disaster (such as an earthquake or flood). It includes emergency response actions, backup operations, and post-disaster recovery.

control

A protective action that a company takes to reduce its risk of exposure.

countermeasure

An action that a company takes to reduce threats to a system. A countermeasure can be a hardware device, software package, procedure, and so on.

data integrity

Ensuring that a company's data has not been exposed to modification or destruction either by accident or from malicious acts.

denial of service

An action or series of actions taken by an intruder. It causes systems to be unavailable for their intended purpose.

easy access

Breaking into a system with minimal effort by exploiting a well-known vulnerability and gaining superuser access in less than 30 seconds (a piece of cake for an intruder).

escalation

The procedure of reporting (and passing responsibility for resolving) a security breach to a higher level of command. See also *internal escalation, external escalation,* and *conflict-of-interest escalation.*

external escalation

The process of reporting a security breach to an individual or group outside the department, division, or company in which it occurred. When a problem is escalated, responsibility for resolving that problem is either accepted or shared with the party to whom the problem is escalated.

exploit

A program or technique that takes advantage of a vulnerability in software and that can be used for breaking security or otherwise attacking a host.

extranet

An extension of a company's intranet to include systems outside the company. An extranet can be used to facilitate easy access to databases and other sources of information between the company and its customers or suppliers. See also *intranet.*

firewall

A security system that controls traffic flow between networks. Several configurations exist: filters (or screens), application relays, encryption, demilitarized zones (DMZ), and so on.

hacker

A person with malicious intentions who gathers information on computer security flaws and breaks into computers without the system owners' permission.

hacking
Exploiting system vulnerabilities to gain unauthorized access.

identification
Recognizing users on a company's systems by using unique names. Not the same as authentication.

incident-response procedures
Formal written procedures that detail the steps to be taken in the event of a major security problem, such as a break-in. Developing detailed incident-response procedures before the occurrence of a problem is a hallmark of a well-designed security system.

internal escalation
The process of reporting a security breach to a higher level of command within the department, division, or company in which the breach occurred.

Internet
The largest collection of networks in the world.

Internet Service Provider (ISP)
The company through which an individual or organization receives access to the Internet. Typically, ISPs provide email service and home page storage in addition to Internet access. Some ISPs also provide offsite data storage and backup services.

intranet
A company's internal network.

ISP
See *Internet Service Provider (ISP)*.

logic bomb
A program that an intruder inserts into software. A logic bomb lies dormant until a predefined condition is met; the program then triggers an unauthorized act.

malicious payload

Typically referred to as "Payload" because it is almost always malicious. Threats can contain programs, often referred to as *payloads*, that perform malicious activities such as denial-of-service attacks, destruction or modification of data, changes to system settings, and information disclosure. Note that the majority of viruses do not contain a payload; they simply replicate.

mass mailer

A threat that self-replicates by sending itself through email. Typically, the threat obtains email addresses by searching for them in files on the system or by responding to messages found in the email client inbox.

password cracker

A software program that tries to match user passwords by using whole dictionaries. (These programs use multiple dictionaries [English French] because many folks just use common words for their passwords.)

password sniffer

See *Snooping tool.*

penetration

The act of gaining unauthorized access to a system or network.

permissions

The authorized actions that a subject can perform with an object (that is, read, write, modify, or delete).

Point of Contact (POC)

The person or persons to whom users or system administrators should immediately report a break-in or suspected security breach. The POC is the information-systems equivalent of a 911 emergency line.

privacy

The protection of a company's data from being accessed by unauthorized parties. Safeguards such as encryption can provide a level of assurance that the integrity of the data is protected from exposure.

reliability

The probability that a system will adequately accomplish its tasks for a specific period of time under the expected operating conditions.

remotely exploitable

Remotely exploitable vulnerabilities are those that can be exploited by attackers across a network. For example, vulnerabilities in web servers that can be exploited by web clients are remotely exploitable vulnerabilities.

risk

The probability that a particular vulnerability of a system will be exploited, either intentionally or accidentally.

risk analysis

A process that determines the magnitude of security risks. A risk analysis identifies controls that need improvement.

security audit

An independent professional security review that tests and examines a company's compliance with existing controls, the results of which enable an auditor to recommend necessary changes in security controls, policies, and procedures.

security procedures

A set of detailed instructions, configurations, and recommendations to implement a company's security policies.

snapshot

A copy of what a computer's memory (primary storage, specific registers, and so on) contains at a specific point in time. Like a photograph, a snapshot can be used to catch intruders by recording information that the hacker might erase before the attack is completed or repelled.

snooping tool

A program that an intruder uses to capture passwords and other data.

spoof

To gain access to a system by masquerading as an authorized user.

threat

Any item that has the potential to compromise the integrity, confidentiality, and availability of data.

tiger team

A group of professional security experts employed by a company to test the effectiveness of security by trying to break in.

time bomb

A program that an intruder inserts into software. It triggers when a particular time is reached or an interval has elapsed.

trap door

See *back door*.

virus

A malicious computer program that needs assistance to spread.

vulnerability

A particular weakness in a company's security policy, system design, installation, or controls that an intruder can exploit.

worm

A program that makes copies of itself on the network from one network disk drive to another or by copying itself using email or another transport mechanism, for example.

Index

J-K-L

M

N

O

P

Q-R

S

T